The Object Lessons series achieves something very close to magic: the books take ordinary—even banal—objects and animate them with a rich history of invention, political struggle, science, and popular mythology. Filled with fascinating details and conveyed in sharp, accessible prose, the books make the everyday world come to life. Be warned: once you've read a few of these, you'll start walking around your house, picking up random objects, and musing aloud: 'I wonder what the story is behind this thing?'"

Steven Johnson, author of *Where Good Ideas Come From* and *How We Got to Now*

Object Lessons describe themselves as 'short, beautiful books,' and to that, I'll say, amen. . . . If you read enough Object Lessons books, you'll fill your head with plenty of trivia to amaze and annoy your friends and loved ones—caution recommended on pontificating on the objects surrounding you. More importantly, though . . . they inspire us to take a second look at parts of the everyday that we've taken for granted. These are not so much lessons about the objects themselves, but opportunities for self-reflection and storytelling. They remind us that we are surrounded by a wondrous world, as long as we care to look."

John Warner, *The Chicago Tribune*

T0205173

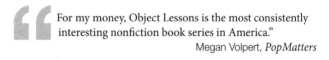

For my money, Object Lessons is the most consistently interesting nonfiction book series in America."

Megan Volpert, *PopMatters*

Besides being beautiful little hand-sized objects themselves, showcasing exceptional writing, the wonder of these books is that they exist at all. . . . Uniformly excellent, engaging, thought-provoking, and informative."

Jennifer Bort Yacovissi,
Washington Independent Review of Books

. . . edifying and entertaining . . . perfect for slipping in a pocket and pulling out when life is on hold."

Sarah Murdoch, *Toronto Star*

[W]itty, thought-provoking, and poetic. . . . These little books are a page-flipper's dream."

John Timpane, *The Philadelphia Inquirer*

Though short, at roughly 25,000 words apiece, these books are anything but slight."

Marina Benjamin, *New Statesman*

OBJECTLESSONS

A book series about the hidden lives of ordinary things.

Series Editors:

Ian Bogost and Christopher Schaberg

Advisory Board:

Sara Ahmed, Jane Bennett, Jeffrey Jerome Cohen, Johanna Drucker, Raiford Guins, Graham Harman, renée hoogland, Pam Houston, Eileen Joy, Douglas Kahn, Daniel Miller, Esther Milne, Timothy Morton, Kathleen Stewart, Nigel Thrift, Rob Walker, Michele White.

In association with

Georgia Tech ⋀ **Center for Media Studies**

BOOKS IN THE SERIES

bulletproof vest

KENNETH R. ROSEN

BLOOMSBURY ACADEMIC
NEW YORK • LONDON • OXFORD • NEW DELHI • SYDNEY

BLOOMSBURY ACADEMIC
Bloomsbury Publishing Inc
1385 Broadway, New York, NY 10018, USA
50 Bedford Square, London, WC1B 3DP, UK

BLOOMSBURY, BLOOMSBURY ACADEMIC and the Diana logo are trademarks
of Bloomsbury Publishing Plc

First published in the United States of America 2020

Library of Congress Cataloging-in-Publication Data
Names: Rosen, Kenneth R., author.
Title: Bulletproof vest / Kenneth R. Rosen.
Description: New York: Bloomsbury Academic, 2020. | Series: Object lessons
| Includes bibliographical references and index. | Summary: "A close
look at an invention with a curious history and influence, an object
that speaks to our notions of, and need for, security in all its
forms"– Provided by publisher.
Identifiers: LCCN 2019040279 | ISBN 9781501353024 (hardback) | ISBN
9781501353031 (epub) | ISBN 9781501353048 (pdf)
Subjects: LCSH: Protective clothing. | Body armor.
Classification: LCC T55.3.P75 R64 2020 | DDC 687/.162–dc23
LC record available at https://lccn.loc.gov/2019040279

ISBN: PB: 978-1-5013-5302-4
ePDF: 978-1-5013-5304-8
eBook: 978-1-5013-5303-1

Series: Object Lessons

Typeset by Deanta Global Publishing Services, Chennai, India
Printed and bound in the United States of America

To find out more about our authors and books visit www.bloomsbury.com and
sign up for our newsletters.

for my wife and son, my armor

"Good men and bad men alike are capable of weakness. The difference is simply that a bad man will be proud all his life of one good deed—while an honest man is hardly aware of his good acts, but remembers a single sin for years on end."

"The greatest tragedy of our age is we don't listen to our consciences. We don't say what we think. We feel one thing and do another."

—VASILY GROSSMAN, WAR CORRESPONDENT (D. 1964)

CONTENTS

PREFACE: NOTES FROM MY SUICIDE

Hiding my past only makes it darker. Here is one of those dark memories and how it came to be. The Smith & Wesson SD40 VE low-capacity handgun looks slick on my coffee table, in my hand, anywhere I place it in my little apartment in Savannah, Georgia. I let the gun hang at my side and stare into a mirror, one five-pound trigger pull away from being a killer, a protector, a hero, someone not to mess with. The weight, a pound and a half, travels up my arm like an extension of my thoughts, an adjunct of power over everything and everyone, including, for once, myself.

I disassemble the weapon. The slide first, then the barrel and chamber with it; a magazine and a spring, and the grip attached to the rail where the slide rests. How simple the construction, how basic the mechanics of death.

I reassemble the gun and fan two ten-round magazines across the table, loading one with a single gold and silver bullet. Another swig of bourbon to make the nerves go down. I close my eyes and pick a magazine. The one with the bullet? Fifty-fifty chances to make things quick. The slicked magazine clicks and engages with the latch inside the handle. The room goes silent. Noel struts around my legs, hops onto my lap, purrs, and buries himself between my thighs. He's always been a loving cat, a trait my mother said he gets from me.

I ease the pistol slide forward. The striker primes. I point the gun away from me and breathe and raise it toward the wall. I disengaged the safety, bring the barrel to my temple, and fire.

At the pawnshop I tell the man I need a pistol for self-defense. I have 200 dollars. He hands me a metal piece. A silver rail, durable black grip. Standing there I feel powerful. Behind him there are bulletproof jackets and flak vest paneling. I find my footing in time and space. I feel grounded. Nothing seems so terrible, but I could also see the end. It was terrible being alive. I consider this my only form of protection.

There was not one big tragedy in my life for which I am blaming my depression. I have seen some things but so had others, worse than me. Sucking it up, I'd long been told, was the proper way to be a man. There were no excuses though I wish I had some. This was my burden, feeling too privileged and like a cliché—a writer who drinks too much, reads Hemingway, and goes and buys a gun. How unoriginal.

Loneliness is a hollow embrace, though sometimes it can be a hedge against more difficult discomfort. It began as something of a small hope against the darkness—knowing how to be alone to get by, a small promise of decompression. But soon I was trapped, the hope inside me faded, and with it I had gone.

Everything about the world is difficult now. Nothing seems possible or worthwhile. Nobody knows this about me because I won't say. And nothing they could say would stop me once I decided to visit this pawnshop.

I'd risen early in the dark of my tiny apartment and readied myself and slipped into the person I was to everyone but me. The person I saw in mirrors wasn't the person I knew. That boy died years ago. That image in the mirror was the only thing left behind. I showed my teeth to the reflection. A crack in the glass ran down the middle and split my head in two. *This could all be over*: this is what I thought as I left my apartment and headed out into the morning, hoping it would be my last.

The pawnshop man says I look like a good kid. He runs a background check and signs the paperwork and tosses the handgun into a brown paper bag. He throws in an extra clip, saying the extra mag is free, and smiles. He says to have a nice day.

Outside the pawnshop, the indifferent world moves about its day. I sip bourbon from a bottle beneath my truck's bench seat and look out over the parking lot at people pushing carts and holding hands. In the fall I will turn twenty-two.

But if I am gone, nothing much will change. What, then, was the point of striving and seeking, never yielding? For what purpose? Why not just lie down? In my absence, the world will still turn. Spring, again, would give way to summer.

I drive through the muggy heat. When I look at the gun inside the brown paper bag on the empty passenger's seat, I realize I've forgotten to buy bullets. Passing under a green light, then a yellow one, then through a red light, I point the white pick-up truck toward another gun shop just off the parkway.

As I drive it bothers me to think about what others might say once I am gone, a growing insecurity making me wish I had also purchased the flak jacket I saw on the wall, if only for something to have that embraces me. I work myself up, thinking about the clichés of suicide—how someone might try to talk me down, how they might say there was so much to live for. Yeah, like what? It was my life and I could choose to do with it what I wanted. How *dare* you. This doesn't *concern* you. All these things I might have said had there been anyone to hold me, to listen.

As it happens, my mother calls me just as I reach the gun and ammo shop. I answer the phone. Her voice lights me up inside; it reminds me I have not always been this way, morose and dark and scared about everything and nothing—both inside and out. I was once unbreakable, never quite this brittle.

I describe to my mother the way of the weather, how this particular day is muggy and unbearable but thank God my air conditioner still works back in the apartment. She asks how the writing life goes and I tell her it goes just fine. "I'm so proud of you. My Kenny, all grown up. Your mother knows best. I always said you'd be some kind of artist. A writer! Wow! You get it from me, you know. The Italian side. Not your father's. He couldn't put together an Ikea set if he tried. Remember your crib I put together all by myself . . ." Yes, I know. I remember. She has told me a thousand times.

She wants to know how Noel, my black and white spotted cat, is doing. She wants to know if he is enough to keep me company and safe and less insecure in my own skin. I say Noel is fine and growing fast—that he misses her; that she should come visit us soon. I don't know why I say that, but she promises that she will.

A box of fifty rounds sets me back twenty dollars. Part of me cringes. The cost of suicide is mounting, not that it matters.

Driving home it seems for all the world as if I am suspended in time. At intersections I pray for a head-on collision. A foreign notion—not "voices" and not unwelcome, perhaps one that has been there all along—tells me it is time to go. Life seems like a Hollywood set, supported by two-by-fours, a gust away from collapse. The traffic light turns green.

For the last time I drive to the beach, where, if you can forgive the ephemeral calm, the restless can find a respite. Waves crash along the shoreline, ebb into fluid greenery, the troubles of a worried mind drifting out to sea, eyelids shut against the bright sun and the sand too hot to touch. The seaweed and oceanic refuse bob under frothy whitecaps. I hate the beach. I can't stand the scantily clothed women with their arms wrapped around large men: women I will never have; men I will never be.

I am convinced it is this sense of loss and lonesomeness and insecurity that is driving me mad. Or is it something else? *Could it be the booze? Had everyone gone because I pushed them away? Was this all my fault? Had I done this to myself?* A couple stroll through the crosswalk and look at me. *Can they hear me?*

Back in my apartment, paint cans, paint rollers, sandpaper, and Spackle litter the floor—here was the evidence of another layer of my hysteria, of me trying to protect and cover up and guard against my past mistakes and fears, fears that seem to grow and spread into larger and less manageable troubles. I'd had a bad trip in the apartment on some tabs of acid I had taken while far too drunk to go any further toward opening my chakras. That night I had returned to this place only to discover that the garish renter's yellow on the walls no longer looked okay. The walls seemed to undulate against an unseen heat wave. And I had to make it *stop*. I knew every paint drop by name.

When I started coming down, I was able to run to a hardware store. On my way back—the world's saturation level turned up to *high*; smells coming to me from long distance—I felt like a cartoon character about to stumble. I had returned with enough supplies to paint four walls, three in a stale blue and an accent wall of deep purple. The walls were riddled with holes from hatchet and knife throwing—loud nights spent alone.

Now back from the beach, I find the hatchet leaning against a wall, its handle sticky with rivulets of paint. Holding the hatchet, I feel light-headed from all the chemicals. Or was it the whiskey? I put the hatchet and gun on the table and recline into my couch. The day is almost over and in a few hours I disengage the safety and bring the barrel to my temple.

When the firing pin engages the room goes dark. My ears ring with the blast and I worry about Noel. Sulfur flits in front of my eyes, but only for a moment. A hole in the Sheetrock of the wall puffs out scarves of smoke. But the only blood comes from my left hand, where the whiskey bottle I held was shattered like the image in a fractured mirror.

The cat. The fucking cat. Where's the fucking cat?

Things fade in and out of view. There is no way I could have missed, but I did. Pulled away at the last second? Chickened out? I'll never know. Divine intervention some might say. Or bad fucking luck. A pinging trails off in my ears and my voice—I can finally hear my voice, but from a distance, calling for Noel.

Here buddy. Come here, buddy. Where the fuck are you? Oh, God . . .

I place the gun on the table and stumble around the apartment, tripping over bottles and books, slipping on papers. Everything is black and white. Everything seems new and distinguished and not my own. I'd entered someone else's apartment. I was an intruder in my own home. I wonder if I have more bourbon, something to keep the room from spinning. I use my hands to find the walls and cling to them like a child to its father. I use my hands to guide me and crawl on my knees. I feel my way around the room until I reach something wet and dripping from the walls.

Noel has knocked over a bucket of purple paint, splattering the wall near the closet, as well as a pile of clothes where he has curled into himself, unharmed, his eyes wide and searching, as though asking me if I have heard that loud bang, too. The walls are ruined, but were they not already? I pick him up and bring him to my chest.

We sit on the floor, rocking together. Maybe I am not exactly alone and maybe there is less to fear than all the intangible worries that led us to this cold floor in an otherwise balmy spring. Noel is there, watching over me, and he seems just fine. What more protection do I need? What else could serve as my protection?

Still, there is evidence to suggest I am alone and still very much vulnerable, as I have been with my thoughts in a place where only my thoughts matter. The only safety meant to keep me whole has otherwise failed. The only safety was in the apartment itself, closed off and indifferent to that world outside, from which no one comes to my knock on my door. No neighbor bangs on the wall or stomps on their floor. I wait for hours and there come no sirens howling from outside, not the slightest movement anywhere at all.

1 EVERY DAY WAS STRIKING

Rockville, Maryland
February 2017

About ten years pass. During that time I pawn my handgun back to the pawnshop and because self-loathing is easily transferable from manifestation in an object to a profession, I become a writer and journalist. Around my nineteenth birthday a reporter for *The New York Times* is freed in a raid by British commandos, but his interpreter—while leading the journalist to rescue—is killed when he emerges from behind a wall, the journalist closely following. Journalists do not carry weapons in war zones, lest they be mistaken for active combatants, though some photojournalists have been mistaken for armed insurgents: an Apache helicopter crew misidentified a shoulder-slung camera as a rocket-propelled grenade. A few years later, in 2014, journalists were beheaded in the sand dunes outside Raqqa, Syria. I wonder if they had wanted their own weapons after they were captured. I wonder if they would have seized a chance to blast their way to freedom in a gunfight. I befriend a writer who was held captive in Somalia and says he almost lunged at a chance to wield a Kalashnikov while in captivity, but ultimately decided against it. Each passing year brought increasing concern to journalists. In 2015, 110 reporters were killed and nearly 200 were jailed worldwide. It's a dangerous job and it is why, whether covering a protest or an active military operation, many chose to wear body armor.

In that rough decade since my salad days, my undergraduate companions were replaced by new classmates who are now, in the winter of 2017 in a suburb of D.C., bound and blindfolded, locked in tiny, ramshackle rooms below the yip-yipping of their captors. We are inside a warehouse, somewhere in the Maryland suburbs, a chorus of car alarms and howling rioters embellishing the realism of this mock-kidnapping and detainment. The sounds inter-stitch with strobe lights for nearly twenty minutes. All I can do is watch. I recuse myself from participating in this portion of the hostile environment training course for journalists and aid workers, in which I enrolled before taking reporting assignments in Iraq. I am not proud of abstaining from the activities at hand. But I cannot shake the angst and anxiety that was woven into me over many years, to say nothing of what it means for me to take an assignment in a war zone thousands of miles away from my rituals of comfort. This class is a prerequisite for reporting in war-torn Mosul, a city in Iraq I will visit in a few weeks as the last fighters of the Islamic State in Iraq and Syria, also known as ISIS or ISIL, are driven out. I have never visited the Middle East. I have never willingly covered an ongoing conflict.

The course instructors—former combat and special forces veterans—stress the importance of becoming a hard target. Never remain still. Never lose focus on your surroundings. Remain ever-vigilant and hyper-focused. It is not so much the course that is useful to me as what it illuminates—I have spent the past decade preparing for extreme, anxiety-inducing situations. I even welcome them. My inconsolable need to check over my shoulder every moment, or the way I jump when someone touches me, the unchecked burden of my past wrongs and worthlessness make sense in a country like Iraq. It's only at home, devoid of those situations, that I have not conquered the hardest part of my disorientation: what to do with silence.

The instructors say nothing of my recusal and offer no signs of concern that I will fly to a war zone ill-prepared. Though, if they do say something, I imagine it might be me responding that this assignment was something I need to do.

My anxiety has gotten to the point of damnable complacency and self-destruction that all but cripples me from social and professional aspirations. If I balk at the chance to cover these stories, then I might as well give into the wretched shell of fear and isolation that have controlled me since that small studio, which now feels forever ago.

Without anything to restrain the strife, the anxiety reappears in ways I'm unable to handle. Some days I shun the world, the feelings so crippling that it seems reasonable to just stay in bed. Inevitably I find myself contemplating how few people would miss me were I to vanish. During these moments, of course, my phone hardly rings, which in turn perpetuates my self-loathing, and I curl back into a ball.

I could blame the root of these feelings of worthlessness on an elementary school crush. Co-ed dances became a thing in elementary school, and I had no luck there. No one would dance with me. But one day, miraculously, someone did agree to a slow dance. I could feel the girl looking over my shoulder as we moved, waiting desperately for the song to end, after which she quickly ran away, back to her friends who surrounded her in a shield of giggles. She had won a bet. Fearing that rejection, I never danced again.

Or perhaps, I might blame my father. He is not a commanding presence, but what he lacks in dominating appearance he makes up for with intelligence. At restaurants he meticulously corrects menus, scanning them for typos with his ballpoint pen. My mother blames him for discouraging my twin sister, Rachele, and me when we were younger, excitable, and eager to share. I'd begin telling a story by saying, "Today me and Rachele—" and my father's stern, low growl of a voice would cut me short, correcting me. "Rachele and I," he'd say, and by then I'd forgotten what I'd wanted to say.

Later still, when I was thirteen years old and attending a military academy, I was often met by physical punishment. Some nights my commanding officers, only seventeen years old themselves, made me assume a push-up position, maintaining it until I collapsed and could not feel my arms. One night, facing a wall, nose pressed against the drywall for hours before my knees buckled, one of them took a sword and shoved it into my back. I wondered if I had invited this behavior. Perhaps they, too, knew of my worthlessness, which is how I became the obvious outlet for their misplaced aggression. Then a sock filled with pennies connected against my head, followed by darkness.

While my patterns of anxiety started young, they slithered into postsecondary school life and a master's degree I couldn't finish. The thought that everyone on campus hated me for the same reasons that I hated myself—because I couldn't formulate, vocalize, and defend an argument without becoming enraged, because I never spoke much and when I did it was only to criticize, because I couldn't handle feedback, because why was a troubled man-child attending the Ivy League—was unbearable. That particular spiral found me standing on a southbound train platform one autumn afternoon, popping anxiety medications, and contemplating what pleasant end would be met at the front of an oncoming subway car.

Thank god for writing and reporting, which helps me straighten these coils into something more manageable. My extroverted work emboldens my introverted self: it grants me brief public achievements that set me on an even keel and save me from a darkly permanent and hermetic life. Otherwise I generally prefer the solitude of my home, where my cat won't confront me about a choice made earlier in my life. I relish the comfort of my squeaky wooden office chair, from which I know my mistakes can be discarded onto the editing room floor and swept away.

Publishing, seeing my name in print or pixels, allows me some self-actualization. I celebrate at each proper paycheck because they mean, in some small way, that I have been somewhere. Someone saw me. I'm not worthless, and neither are the stories I write. The checks are my hedge against the twitch of anxiety that tells me to stay indoors and placate my inherent worries with solitude.

It's this need to push myself out into the open that has caused me, for example, to chaperone a man who tried to mug me at gunpoint in Georgia. He needed a lift to his girlfriend's house and since I didn't have any cash, I offered him a ride and a chance to tell me his story. This is also how, as one of my early beat reporting assignments, I landed in Alaska on a damp spring evening after flying into the airport sideways and barely landing, my excitement pounding through my chest.

My heart ripples through my chest, hooked by the sight of my classmates curled into admissions of defeat, their bodies like white rags of surrender flapping at the breeze and the actors who are terrorists screaming in their ears. At the end of the class I purchase a medical kit—QuikClot hemostatic blood agent, trauma shears, Band-Aids, gauze, and alcohol prep wipes—and feel that if there is one thing I treasure most from this class it is this kit. My personal security grows with the things I carry, the places I have been, and the people I meet.

Building ahead of my trip, the medical kit adds to my growing collection of tools and equipment at home that serve to bring comfort on the battlefield. A mix between retail and practical therapy, I go overboard during an Amazon shopping spree, and I now have splayed out in my home office in Brooklyn what I will bring on my first trip to Iraq: my personal cellphone and a secondary cellphone and a GPS tracking device and a burner laptop and travel power outlet adapters and Sharpies and pens and maps and cash in several currencies and travel documents and antidiarrheal pills and a prescription for Azithromycin, to aid me in the event I drink unsanitary water, which rattles next to a full bottle of over-the-counter sleep medication, enough to anesthetize a gorilla. Still, I pack foam earplugs.

I call my friend seeking advice. He has just returned from Mosul. He tells me to never stand still, like the class taught me. He says be careful of snipers. The members of ISIS are a good shot, regardless of what they say in the media. I call another friend, *The New York Times* Baghdad bureau chief. I ask him a question that has been troubling me since I was assigned the story. Do I need body armor? He says yes, but to keep it in the trunk. The next question I ask is silly and ridiculous: How will I know when to use the flak jacket and helmet? His answer amounts to, "you'll know," as though it was a choice when someone wanted to be safe and when they were willing to risk the absence of the protective vest.

He made it sound like casually deciding when to unpack a duvet for winter.

The shopping spree continues because clicking "Buy Now" is an uninhibited catharsis. How liberating it is to choose something you want and simply, instantly, it becomes yours. I also begin shopping for tactical combat helmets and flak jackets online. I have been reading the memoir of a photojournalist in which she mentions the retailer where she purchased her first set of PPE, or personal protective equipment: bulletproofme.com.

They are based in Texas and tell me that there are several types of protection, rated by the National Institute of Justice, which provides the standards for several body-armor protective types used by police and military. The type of ballistic performance of each armor panel—though the plates, or panels, themselves are placed often within synthetic or fabric "plate carriers"—are combined to different standards of ballistic survivability.

Type IIA and Type II can withstand 9 mm and .40 mm Smith & Wesson Full Metal Jacket rounds and .357 Magnum rounds, respectively, all of which are fairly common handgun calibers used by everyone from active shooters to your local law enforcement officers. Type III can come in a plate carrier or be the rating of an actual plate inserted into an unrated or stab-proof-only plate carrier, meant to be used to deter stab wounds but also used by physical trainers who load the pockets not with bulletproofing but with lead weights. The Type IIIA stops threats such as .357 SIGs and .44 Magnums, heavier handgun calibers used in pistols such as the Desert Eagle. Type III can stop six rounds of a 7.62 x 51 mm known colloquially as the 7.62 NATO because of its use in rifles by allied countries. The 7.62 NATO is the military version of the .308 Winchester Full Metal Jacket, a popular hunting round used to kill whitetailed deer, pronghorn, caribou, elk, or black bear. Type IV, which may also come as a plate carrier, and can withstand a single .30-06 Armor-Piercing round alongside at least a single hit from a .308, AK-47, and other Type I through III calibers.

While placing my order on the phone, I spend less time concerned about the protection type than the color. (I choose a ProMAX Tactical, non-concealable Type IV plate carrier, which can accommodate front and rear Type IIIA lightweight ceramic rifle plates, meant to withstand not one, but two .30-08 armor-piercing rounds.)

"Usually journalists go with our blue variation with a white-letter PRESS patch," Nick, the salesman, tells me over the phone.

"Yeah, I get that, and they also have the groin and neck protectors," I say, "but blue . . . in the desert . . ."

"Yeah," Nick says, "I get your point. You'll stick out with all that sand. Where are you going, again?" I tell him Iraq. "Ah, yeah, then maybe you wanna go tan rather than blue. We also have black."

"Black sounds, too—I'm not sure—commando?"

"Tan it is," he says. (It is still many weeks before I learned that the blue is *meant* to stand out, to show that the wearer is not a combatant in the military but rather media apart from the fighting.)

"Do I need to match the helmet?"

"I'm not sure what you mean," he says.

I'm too embarrassed to say I wonder whether I should match my Type IIIA NATO combat fragmentation helmet with the color of my vest and simply order black. I figure I can spray paint it later.

I nervously wait for the package to arrive, counting down the weeks, then days, until my trip. It finally arrives ten days before my plane departs for Erbil, in Northern Iraq.

The vest and helmet arrive in a large package. I tear off the tape and peel back the corrugated sections of the box to reveal four plastic bags. In one bag there is the PRESS patch, in another the rifle plates, in another the helmet, and, in the last, the bulletproof vest. I stop dead, disappointed and flummoxed. There are clips and straps on the side, which make the vest bulky and look more like a special operator's gear. I thought I had ordered something concealable. I wanted something I could wear without anyone knowing, appearing full of machismo though really terrified and trembling beneath the weight of the vest. Before I call Nick, I unlatch the Velcro pouches in the front and back of the vest and slide the ceramic plates into the vest and pull the ensemble over my head. I buckle the clasps, cinch tight the Velcro rib bands. I go into the bathroom and take a look. It fits, but it is my eyes that are bulging. I snap a photo and send to my friend Brett, one of the very few people who knows I'm heading overseas.

"You look terrified," he says in a text message. I am.

I call Nick and tell him that I believe my bulletproof vest is the wrong one, that they have sent me the wrong version. He calls my set my PPE, a phrase which seemed to distance me still from the purpose of this purchase. I simply continued preferring to call it my bulletproof vest and helmet. He says that cannot be and checks the order and that there's something that might have gotten messed up on his end and asks if I want to replace the order. I tell him I can't, that my trip is in a few days. He says that he is sorry and wishes me luck.

Then, before we hang up, he tells me something that for all the world does nothing to abate my anxiety. "And don't forget," Nick says. "Nothing's bullet*proof*. The thing's only bullet *resistant*."

2 A THIN METAL SHEET

When I first arrive in Iraq I know the downtime will be the most difficult—a mental and emotional trap through which I know I must find ways to bide my time to feel secure. The Tigris River stands to my right as we move closer to a checkpoint ahead. Dark clouds from rubbish fires surround the car in which I am alone with two men I hardly know and who I can hardly understand, because I do not speak Kurdish or Arabic, only English, and they seem less enthused about speaking English only for my benefit. I feel eclipsed by this moment, fears that exist in not being able to communicate or understand, as though I am being reborn.

We are at a standstill not far outside the liberated city of Mosul. What I worry about most is whether or not I will return home with the stories I set out to write. I worry about my mother and sister discovering that I have ventured into a war zone without any real knowledge of the region or for my safety beyond the quick course I took in Maryland. I worry that I am dressed inappropriately. I worry that maybe

I am dressed too much like a tourist, or that I don't have the clothes meant for the region, or that I haven't packed enough to compensate for changes in weather. I worry that someone might know, by virtue of my last name, that I am a Jew. I worry about my colleagues based here, if they think less of me for having parachuted into their country without knowing the nuances of the people or situation here. I fret that the concierge at one of the hotels in Erbil, the capital of the Kurdish region in Northern Iraq, despises me for asking him to watch my stuff while I visit the front line for a few days. I stew in the knowledge that nearly six thousand miles could not divorce me from my most basic of worries: everything. I try everything to keep from thinking I am failing at reporting, failing at gathering enough information for the story. I, despite continuing stories about vehicle-borne, improvised explosive devices and snipers, never worry about death.

I swear I hear my fixer and driver say Deash, the Arabic acronym for ISIS. I believe they are planning to sell me to some stranger in the desert. Of course, they could be talking about the war we are covering, but I do not want to take a chance on presumptions, tossing my fate into the hands of unreliable protection that, at best, is mine to control. So I interrupt their conversation and tell them that I am meeting a security detail in Erbil in three hours and must be there on time. It is my first time alone with them, without the photographer assigned to the stories, Sandra, as my ears and barrier between the war and me. All I had really done, after watching Sandra scramble out from the car earlier, leaving the door open behind her, was to email my father to say that if he did not hear from me in three hours to follow the emergency contingency plan. He wrote, "OK." And my nerves abated somewhat.

I feel that same feeling of complete entrapment as I had once before in a car with a stranger, knowing that I knew not where I was nor where exactly I was going, but this time my phone is not dead, and I have with me my GPS tracker. I know people in the area and am, above all, sober and cognizant. So I take note of the worry and push it elsewhere, aside, to a place that will not tie me down but instead free me up to react and not implode. How worthless the PPE, seated nearby, seems. One of the largest problems in any foreign country, especially in one that is experiencing constant violence, is kidnapping, second to fatal car accidents. I'm not convinced the flimsy ceramic plates tucked into a vest in the trunk will help me with either of those.

When finally we reach an area from which I can make a phone call, I share some of my reporting concerns with my editor, a dear friend.

She tells me to trust myself, that I have reported before, and that I should go in whatever direction the story takes me. I like to think she knows what I do: focusing elsewhere was the only way to move forward. Pointing the lens outward would allow me to heal my inner disruption. Focusing on things outside my control would only cinch tighter my perception of the people and this place. It would cause me insurmountable insecurity.

Yet, still in the trunk and within reach, I have my body armor behind which sat those two ceramic plates twice the thickness of my thumb and I wonder how such a curious lace could bring me such comfort—despite the existential worries about everything other than a Kalashnikov or rocket-propelled grenade—given the assurance of a deadly projectile.

The history of weapons and defense against weapons predate recorded human history. Human evolution demanded a solution to its own vulnerability. A weak species must arm itself for any chance at survival against predatory factions—humans or other mammals—throughout its nomadic travels.

One of the earliest weapons systems, used at first for hunting, were stone tips affixed to spears and arrows. Bone and stone tools used to fashion spearheads and arrowheads were discovered in sites inhabited by indigenous North Americans and the African Pleistocene tribes, some dating more than 60,000 years ago, such as an arrowhead found in modern-day South Africa.

But as stone-tipped arrowheads were eventually replaced by bronze to include use as spearheads, and as civilization was born in southern Mesopotamia in 4,000 BCE, the Sumerians shifted the use of such weaponry from hunting to protection. The birth of civilization meant fixed agrarian communities would need more than just weapons to fetch meals, but also to protect against invasion.

Early Sumerian city-states constantly at war with each other, in what is now the Fertile Crescent of present-day Iraq, were vulnerable to enemy invasion. Bronze weapons such as socket axes were insufficient by themselves for Sumerian warriors. Knowing this, metal workers at the time created copper helmets, forged to withstand the impact of flying projectiles and anything aimed at human perforation.

As the smiths' technical knowledge of weapons and war machines and their defensive uses grew, so too did their knowledge of circumventing safety allow them to imagine more nuanced offensive weaponry. Sumerians preferred axes to maces, the former being a more effective piercing agent and more likely to puncture helmets with their leveraged and pointed ends. Craftsmen continued fortifying the helmets against advances in forgery and blades. The Sumerians had begun what became a necessary study of war: how to build the most lethal weaponry and how to develop the defensive measures used to stop them.

This tug-of-war between what was meant to protect and defend, to attack and confront, an inherent battle between self-preservation by doing and by not doing, is a defining element in the evolution of humankind and civilization. For one, it was important that a people or a person knew how to defend themselves. Oftentimes it meant being able to attack, to initiate the offensive and surprise enemies. Protecting one's own family, tribe, or nation was also rightly conflated with the necessity to not merely build walls but also to defend those walls. Many times, it was advantageous to defend those walls before they were ever breached, and thus advanced weaponry and the systems used to shoulder them—the bodywear that made the operators better suited to combat situations—were born.

The oldest-known Western full-body armor dates to the Mycenaean period of Greek history, between 1600 and 1100 BCE, at least 60,000 years after the oldest weapons were around and 1,600 years after the first Sumerian-created helmets. Known as the Dendra panoply, it is the earliest example of a bronze "cuirass" comprised of large metal plates: a piece of body armor consisting of a breastplate and backplate fastened into a single garment. The armor also had plates to cover and protect the shoulders, armpits, neck, and shins of the warriors who wore it. Classicists debate whether the armor was designed to protect charioteers or spearmen, who, in addition to the heavy protective gear, carried "eight- to ten-foot thrusting spears" and massive wooden shields. This design was later abandoned in favor of clothing better suited for fast-paced combat—linen and simple shields were more cost-efficient and less restrictive to movement and agility, improving the dexterity needed to wield a spear.

The Mycenaean's approach to warfare at that time evolved from a compromise between protection and mobility. Layers of protection were seen as essential to thwarting enemies—but not at the cost of one's own mobility. To attack the soldier in hand-to-hand combat, an enemy would first have to get through a horse, a chariot, and leather armor reinforced with plates of bronze. Things and protectors were placed between one's fear and reality. The distance to travel from worrier to warrior was shortened.

To better equip these warriors for a close-range melee, Mycenaean soldiers were also given boar-tusk helmets, an archetypal token from the period. These helmets are named literally, with the tusks of these animals shaped into small pieces and fashioned along equidistant rows and can be found littered throughout the fields of the Trojan War and throughout the lines of Homer's telling of the battle. Unlike these helmets, unique to the Greeks, cuirasses were increasingly common in many armies for several centuries to come. The Romans chose to make theirs out of iron as opposed to the bronze used by the Greeks.

The Romans also began incorporating chain mail into their armored gear. The earliest record of chain mail was found in Celtic graves dating to 400 BCE. By some accounts, the Romans encountered the armor in battle with the Celts around 390 BC. Constructed of tiny, interlocking metal rings, which took smiths weeks and sometimes months to complete, the chain mail formed a nearly impenetrable layer that was lighter in weight than bronze and allowed the user a free range of motion. Chain mail covered large parts of a soldier's body at less expense to their maneuverability. The use of unskilled labor to produce mail compared to the more expensive blacksmiths for plated armor and its relatively one-size-fits-all nature, made it more accessible to the common foot soldier. Chain mail itself could also be easily repaired given the relatively simple design behind it.

By the Middle Ages and the Renaissance period, chain mail would be adapted to make various garments, from shirts of various lengths, to leggings, hoods, mittens, and collars.

But a soldier couldn't wear only chain mail, which was often used as a warrior's liner or under-armor (and later the inspiration, perhaps, for the athletic clothing line called UnderArmour). The linked design was often employed beneath those suits of armor or other heavy panels. Common foot soldiers would use a heavy cloth or canvas garment—called a brigandine—over a chain-mail shirt. Brigandines were vest-like body armor, similar to a cuirass in shape and designed to protect the torso from various angles. Unlike the cuirass, though, the predominant material was the canvas with secondary, smaller metal plates riveted to the garment. The design of brigandines is comparable to the scale armor and lamellar armor that had existed in eastern Europe and different areas of Asia. Scale armor consisted of individual plates of various materials sewn in overlapping rows in a way that looked like scales on reptiles or fish. The material used depended on available resources, such as bronze, iron, and leather. This armor could handle piercing and blunt attacks better than chain mail, but it lacked flexibility.

Certain versions of lamellar armor, used by Japanese samurai in the Heian period (794 CE–1185 CE) were similar in principle to scale armor, but small rectangular plates of wood or leather laced together. Minor adjustments in the types of scales used on the armor and the substances used to tie them together were made over time, but by the end of this period, the style of the Japanese lamellar armor was recognizably samurai, which rose to be in the vanguard of body-armor designers for several centuries.

The relative stagnation of armor development at the time did not stop the evolution of weapons. Chain mail's disadvantages were becoming easier to exploit. Blunt force weapons such as war hammers could cause harm without needing to pierce through the armor. The flexible mail could also injure the wearer if compromised in combat.

It was not until the 1300s that chain mail was once again supplemented with plated armor in order to combat the advanced weaponry. The two were incorporated into a single armor, called plated mail, in which plate armor was used to cover essential parts of the body including the head, torso, limbs, and large joints. This armor could be supplanted by the complete suit of armor typically associated with medieval knights. By the mid-15th century chain mail was relegated to an under-armor.

Altogether, a full plate-mail armor system could weigh from 15 to 25 kg, or about 33 to 55 lbs. In comparison, a hauberk, which is the knee-length chain-mail shirt, weighs roughly 10 kg, or 22 lbs.

Armor, in all its iterations, was designed for battle, but it had more than just a functional purpose; the aesthetic of a soldier in their armor for the sake of pageantry was not unheard of. During parades and tournaments, royalty and nobility would don their customized, decorated armor suits. The intricacies of armor from that era lent itself to being mistaken as decorative flourish to begin with. In some cases, the armor was made specifically for short-term, exhibitionist purposes. Such was the case with the jousting armor in the 15th and 16th centuries. The suits of armor donned by horsemen for jousting in tournaments weighed 50 kg (110 lbs.), much heavier than that typically used in combat.

By the 1500s, with the advent of gunpowder, the Samurai began using an armor known as Tosei-gusoku. Similar to the armor of a medieval knight, Tosei-gusoku used metal plates to protect essential body parts such as the head, torso, and limbs. By the 1540s, the Portuguese brought a perfected recipe for gunpowder alongside matchlock muskets for trade. Ball-bearing-sized dents in plated armor proved their bullet-resistant properties to would-be wearers.

The firearms also gave Europeans a distinct advantage when it came to colonizing North and South America against native populations, who had had little use for sophisticated body armor. For those native populations, there had been no rise and fall of the Holy Roman Empire, no Dark Ages, and no Renaissance in the New World. The tribal indigenous nations inhabiting the Americas had developed weapons and defensive equipment in a different manner. Unlike the metallic armors long the norm in European armies, the Aztec warriors who dominated parts of present-day Mexico used cotton. Protection often changes, though, and what once kept at bay certain demons did not always deter other, unknown, demons.

The Aztecs soaked quilted cotton in a saltwater brine, which crystallized when dried. The garment stiffened enough that when layered it could protect warriors from blades and spears. When these warriors were called to battle, they would fight with weapons forged from obsidian, a glass-like rock found in the solidified lava of neighboring volcanoes—and a shield. Helmets were carved in the shapes of animals to represent a warrior's tribe, their people, for whom they were fighting.

Perhaps the most distinctive quality of Aztecan warfare was an inherent desire to avoid violence, typified not only by their acceptance of death and lack of body protection, but by their willingness to negotiate for peace. They never attacked by surprise. Their goal was never to eliminate their opponent. They understood that protections in a dangerous world were necessary, but not always needed. A desire toward harmony, a penchant for empathy and understanding, was often the greatest form of defense.

And yet.

Not all things can be defended against. With their advanced weaponry the Europeans had brought with them diseases that had never before been introduced to the New World. European nations had conquered and divided North and South America because their greatest defense was their offense. They didn't need protection from the natives so much as the natives needed protection from the colonizers. No cotton or helmet or shield could protect against something unseen and invisible.

In the intervening years it seemed then this became more acknowledged by commanders and conquerors. There was little use in protecting troops when what generals most cherished were speed and numbers.

Kazimierz Żegleń (Casimir Zeglen), a Polish monk born in 1869 near Tarnopol (died in 1927 or later), invented one of the first bulletproof vests. At the age of eighteen he entered the Resurrectionist Order in Lwów (today Lviv, Ukraine). In 1890, he moved to the United States.

It wasn't the first attempt at a bulletproof vest using a non-bulletproof material. The Myeonje baegab, a vest from Korea made of layers of cotton, was known to thwart bullets at least two decades prior.

Civil, foreign and world wars were fought in a period when even the toughest armor could not stop the most lethal weapon. In this period, it is observed that protective gear was greatly scaled back, retreating once more from full-body armor to strategically placed metal plates. To protect against gunfire, as battlefields grew farther apart and cannon fire spelled imminent death, as the fighting grew less personal and more distanced (like the relationship between the men who called the orders to those who marched to them), men wore metal plates over their uniforms and donned metal helmets. These plates were placed over the heart, which often beat with a fear that was hardly aided by the presence of a thin metal sheet and, later, a fabric known as Kevlar.

3 ENJOY THE WAR

Mosul, Iraq
April 2017

As a young boy, for the Jewish holiday of Purim celebrated at the yeshiva and synagogue I attended in those days, I once constructed a costume out of Ticonderoga pencils. The holiday commemorates the saving of the Jewish people from Haman, an Achaemenid Persian Empire official who was planning to kill all the Jews. We children dressed up as an allusion to the nature of the Purim miracle, where the details of the story are really miracles hidden within natural events that led to the Jews' survival. I hardly knew this then and only wished to be a warrior, like one of the Maccabees who saved my people from certain slaughter, so I strung together (wasted, really) dozens of Ticonderoga #2 pencils, wrapping them with Scotch tape into plates of armor, which I fastened around my arms, torso, and legs.

Many years later, my real bulletproof plating is as thick as hell. I keep it always in reach as we drive, meaning while it is in the trunk I still have access to it through the hatchback. It's a tough, harsh, and abrasive fabric that I love to touch. I try not to stay too far from the vest and helmet in the back of the vehicle when we stop to conduct interviews. I begin to split my attention during the interviews, between the people who are telling me about the coalition airstrikes that destroyed their houses, or the residents of Eastern Mosul who are offering me a cup of tea and between the thoughts of the vest and plates. My mind is divided between the two and, rather than focus, I am virtually absent from these conversations. My mind splits further when we traverse a rocky canyon and follow tight rabbit trails, minding our steps for land mines: partly thinking of my vest and its effectiveness, partly of what people are telling me, and partly whether or not I should worry about something exploding at my feet. A major (or is he a colonel?) compliments me on my vest one afternoon and asks if I am willing to trade him for his own set. His is bulkier, more battered. I smile and decline, hooking my hands into the neckline of my own, realizing how vulnerable I am at the jugular.

Of course, no vest can protect me from my religion. I am prepared every time I am asked. I am Christian, I say. Many soldiers—at checkpoints, on rooftops, looking down the iron sights of an assault rifle—tell me I look Iraqi and ask where I am from. I tell them I am from the US, and then they ask me if I am Lebanese. I realize they are close in their estimation. I have a dark-skin and look as though I have arrived straight from Tel-Aviv, the way I looked at in my early days of tutelage at yeshiva. Years later I would make friends in Iraq and still be too frightened to say I am a Jew.

Each night the freelance journalists covering the battle for Mosul return to the city of Erbil, about three hours east of the fighting. The city's an epic reprieve. The streets are deserted, but foreigners litter the few bars and restaurants in the Christian neighborhood of Ankawa. Comfort and protection exist in many forms, mainly alcohol, which is one way to elide any fear or worry that arose from what was reported or seen in the city throughout the day. For me, my routine involves the comforts of home: food and a bed, displacement from everyone and everything, and a good book or journal into which I can invest myself. So I order beef shawarma sandwiches and bottles of water, which I greedily fill with electrolyte packages. The fruit drink and meat do not mix well, but I'm thankful to be eating virtual room service within a war zone. The sleeping pills, which I pluck from my med kit, ease me into a dreamy sleep and the celebratory gunfire outside retreats with the imam calling residents to prayer a few blocks over in the Muslim neighborhood.

In the morning I wake up and struggle down to the lobby, lugging with me my helmet, body armor, and my backpack filled with everything I've brought: my med kit, clothes, electrolyte packages, water bottles, gas mask. I order a small Turkish coffee. Alone in the lobby, I look past the metal detector and stare into the street, waiting for my fixer and driver to arrive. It's the second day of reporting and after having driven with them yesterday, having seen how long they left me to struggle in my head alone with my thoughts in a strange country wracked by war, I have begun to secretly loathe them. Sandra sends me a text message to say that the fixer and driver are late to picking her up—they sped back home last night, two hours outside the city, to party with friends. They are now hungover and running late. My patience wears thin. I order another coffee. I can't seem to feel anything but helpless. We have an appointment at nine to meet with the convoy heading into the city and we are sure to miss that now. I have all this gear, and for what?

Despite all the equipment, there are some things over which I simply have no control. The designs of others are not something I can manipulate, better I try to be a good manager and organizer. I let the anger wash over me, a disappointment that nothing in my gear bag can alleviate. I breathe deep and enjoy the coffee. It is hot and gritty and I'm thankful for Sandra, who is my virtual companion. We exchange text messages while we wait.

She is a savior. We met briefly after I arrived—jet-lagged, my head swimming from restlessness and worry. I sat with my back to the glass facade of the lobby in which we first met. It is where we also met the fixer who was now AWOL. I tried to take charge then as best I could, outlining our reporting plan and my expectations from the fixer: I wanted him to be punctual, and I gave him a list of the people I wanted to speak with and a list of the places we wanted to visit. He said, with nodding and thoughtful approval, that this would be a cinch. He knew the perfect driver.

We spent our first day not reporting but haggling with several Iraqi special forces soldiers who manned a checkpoint to the southwest of Mosul. Sandra tried to retrieve her bulletproof plate carrier—one made by 5.11 Tactical, which turned out to be the preeminent brand in the Middle East, used by journalists and military alike, as though the protective wear's main purpose itself was to be fashionable—from the front line where she served as a medic and photographer. She had left it with her boyfriend, Max. But on that day we had no luck getting through.

The driver, as we waited, leaned over to Sandra. He had made eyes and small talk with her throughout the drive. She is very pretty. Blonde hair, blue eyes. For Iraq, she is exotic. As he leaned over, he said in Arabic, "If you are naked, we could go anywhere." She laughed uncomfortably and translated for me. I said nothing, a choice not to act which I would return for many despairing nights. The fixer looked at me and Sandra and told us not take it personally. He said the driver was kidding. I stared out the window, dumbly and afraid.

I felt uncomfortable, as though we were already doing everything wrong and that I should have asserted myself somewhere along the way but I hadn't and that itself might have prevented our slow start, if not the disresepect. At a nearby shack converted into a military outpost, over a lunch of yogurt, served to us from a ten-gallon bucket, a soldier asked me where I was from. I told him New York City. My fixer told him I was from *The New York Times*.

"*New . . . York . . . Times?*" The solder said, arching his eyebrows.

I smiled and he reached for his phone. A few thumb and finger gestures later, he was showing me a selfie he had taken. It showed him with his arms around a friend of mine who had worked in the region for close to a decade. Seeing his face eased me: he must have gone through similar bureaucratic stalling, of logistical nightmares like this. It was part of the reporting, this kind of correspondence. I smiled, sitting with my back against a wall to which my T-shirt stuck in the summer heat. Sandra was fluent in Arabic, having worked and lived in the region for three years. She was an easy presence around tough men. She didn't seem to need a vest.

We returned to Erbil that afternoon.

That was yesterday. Now I find myself waiting for the fixer and his driver, sipping coffee in the lobby as Sandra and I trade messages. She tells me they just arrived at her apartment so I trudge outside to wait for their car. An old Toyota Prado pulls up. Its seats are covered with wood beads and fabrics. I toss my gear bag, helmet, and bulletproof vest into the hatchback. My PPE. Some use it'll be back there, so when I climb into the back seat with Sandra, I reach into the rear and pull forward the vest, placing it near the door panel nearest me. It's something I learned at that training course: in case of armed assailants, place your vest against the door and crouch behind it. I'm six foot two, and inflexible, making this arrangement mostly worthless.

Sandra and I discuss our story, about how Iraqi forces are treating the bodies of dead ISIS fighters. We figure we'd start outside the city, since now we'd be late and miss the convoy to the inner city and frontline, where some of the most intense fighting is occurring between Iraqi Federal Police, ISOF (Iraqi Special Operations Forces), and ISIS. The fighting, in Mosul's Old City on the western banks of the Tigris River, is being compared to urban combat throughout World War II. I don't know how the fighting will pan out, but I believe I have the necessary gear.

After a two-hour drive, through countless checkpoints through which my fixer alternately yells "War Media!" and "*New York Times* journalist!" we reach the staging area outside Mosul where we should have linked with units from the Federal Police. The dirt lot in which we stand is filled with debris. It is off a main road along which convoys of United Nations Development Programme (UNDP) vehicles and armored Toyota Hi-Lux pick-up trucks carry international aid workers between camps filled with internally displaced people. The war machine is well oiled and in high gear.

Children kick a soccer ball along the far end of the street. They shout and scream and giggle between the dust clouds kicked up by passing military Humvees. The Humvees are bullet-ridden and stitched with crude plates of metal used for armor. Heavy machine guns are welded to different exterior locations: on the backs of flatbed trucks or pick-ups, in Humvees, in simple sedans converted specifically for the work of killing or defense, a matter of semantics.

One of the white pick-up trucks speeding along the revs its engine higher. The truck is barreling toward us, then careens to a stop several yards from where we're standing. Worried, ever cautious, I feel for my bag and the body armor and reposition myself nearest the engine block of our truck. I'm told this is where to hide when being shot at. The density and construction of the engine and the rear axle make for good hiding spaces if ever you find yourself under siege. Thinking about this, I feel pathetically small and edgy.

Sandra is standing outside and smiles at the truck as a burly man with a small gut alights and makes his way toward us. He is American: a baseball cap with the American flag flying backward sits atop his head. He replaced the hat with a hand which he combs through his black hair. This is Max, a frontline medic and former military infantryman. He's come to Iraq to start a business and work on the frontline tending to wounded soldiers and civilians. His demeanor is calm, collected. He wears a T-shirt and Oakley sunglasses and smiles through a wispy beard. His arms are covered in tattoos, like mine, but he has one spot that is covered by a large Band-Aid.

Sandra and Max say hello to one another.

"Want a Wild Tiger?"

"Yeah, I could use it right now," I say, reaching for the energy drink he plucked from the truck bed. "Coffee in the hotel isn't quite doing it."

"Sounds about right."

Sandra tells him about our story, how we're trying to find the dead bodies of ISIS fighters to see what became of them after they fell fighting to defend their self-proclaimed caliphate. He laughs and says they are worthless, those fighters, and for all he's seen of the damage they inflict—on themselves, on the people of Iraq and Mosul, on young children—they aren't worth being cared for or sought after.

"Someone needs to be nice to them," Sandra says. I agree. It seems that if the rules of engagement are anything to abide, we should know that all parties to a conflict deserve the same dignified end. Each side is fighting for its own justifiable position. Each side is chasing in its view an honorable objective and dominance against what it sees as evil, a way to overcome or attain something that would, in more ways than I can express while standing in this field, lead them to peace and security.

From where we stand we see towering clouds of black smoke, remnants of oil-field fires set by ISIS. The plaintive fields of tall grass—for which the "breadbasket of civilization" in Northern Iraq, is best known—are a blur beneath the smoke outside Mosul. I'm nervous about getting into the city, nervous standing here, in the lot outside a Federal Police base that was, only two days ago, attacked by an ISIS sleeper cell from the village where the children are playing soccer. I look across a berm that shoulders a drainage ditch and wonder who might be looking at me and through what—a scope? Binoculars? A machine-gun nest and Iraqi flag in the distance overlooked a hill. I never imagined I'd find comfort in the sight of their red and black flag—it beat the hell out of seeing an ISIS flag. When we passed the village outside earlier, before turning into the lot, the young children had thrown up the hand signal of ISIS, showing their support. They likely knew not what the single finger raised meant. They likely believed it was some gag, but it shook me. I remember their gestures now, standing here, thinking that this one small battle will mean nothing, and those who die here—the reporters, the civilians, the soldiers—will be buried beneath sand and earth, forgotten.

My concentration is broken by Max who is talking coolly about the makeshift hospital he was working at earlier in the day. Sandra is looking at him with awe. I point out the Band-Aid on his tattooed arm and Sandra says she'll tell me later. She does not want to say anything about it in front of our fixer and Max gets into his truck.

"Well," he says pulling closed the driver-side door, "enjoy the war!"

He turns the truck around and heads back onto the road, along which there are guards, and bases, and more internally displaced persons' camps, and UN agencies, and soldiers, and all the infrastructure of war that lends itself to an air of efficiency if not operational security. There is safety in numbers, it is said. I think back to the conversation I had with my friend and the bureau chief who told me to never stay still, always keep moving, to always note the demeanor of my fixers. I bobbed my head like a boxer, avoiding potential snipers despite the way my fixer and Sandra are relaxing against the car, basking in the sun. Silly, the things we do to keep ourselves moving forward.

Finally our ride is here, but the ranking officer says he cannot take us to Mosul, so I begin to fidget and beg my fixer to get us moving. He complains to the ranking officer who shakes his head, saying in Arabic that he just can't help as we have arrived too late. I kick dirt and ask if we can at the very least see a few dead bodies. I am tired of trying to be anything other than direct. It seems to me the best way to handle the safety of my team—Sandra, the fixer, and the driver—is to say what we need and how we plan to get that with this officer's help, transparency and frankness becoming an olive branch.

Sandra approaches the ranking officer and pleads our case in Arabic, but the driver shoots back that the woman should stay in the car. I tell the fixer to translate for me. He repeats what Sandra said and then what the driver said. I am furious and tell him to tell the driver to get back in the car and to stay there. I tell the fixer that he needs to relay the following to the driver: that he is to drive, nothing more. The wheel is where he should stay, with his mouth shut, and the fixer agrees.

The ranking officer says the convoy is gone and that we cannot go anywhere without an escort. I say this is fine, we will take our own car. He says it is too dangerous. I say we are fine, that we have our gear and we must go to do our mission, using a word I think he will associate with rank and chain of command, telling him my editor is demanding it and that I must go, or I will not complete my objective. He starts to understand and says he can spare a Humvee to accompany us to Albu Saif, on the outskirts of the city by the airport.

We clamber into our Toyota and wait for the escort. I look around to see if Sandra or the fixer or diver are putting on their body armor, their personal protective equipment, but no one flinches.

While we are sitting in the heat, I rest a cigarette between my lips and roll down the back passenger window. The sun is bearing down on my thighs. I stick to everything. The car is off, and the only cool air comes from the lowered windows. I light my cigarette. I hate the driver. I ask Sandra whether she thinks people are born good or bad. Most, she believes, are born good. I tell her I think people are born inherently good, but it takes only one small thing to turn them bad. Being good is a choice, I say, being bad is a rather easy default. After a taste of evil it's easier to be bad than return to good. It's a fight to stay human, to remain concerned. I am blathering nervously, diverting my attention from my frustration and discomfort.

We talk for a little while about the different acronyms fighting to liberate Mosul— Federal Police, ISOF, or various militias—and soon a Humvee directs us to follow it and we do.

Along the road I am always looking ahead, wondering whether that crumpled piece of trash is hiding a roadside bomb. I try to comfort myself that there would likely be no munitions in an area heavily trafficked by the Iraqi military, with them having cleared this area long go. I try to comfort myself in this thought, only to remember that the sleeper cells around Mosul are getting more daring and craftier. A nighttime journey to this area to place a bomb would not be unheard of.

We take a turn and navigate through a small pass between dirt hills. A row of train tracks sits on the horizon, connecting two more small dirt hills. To our right and left are deep wadis, or valleys, filled with the debris of war and refuse from the nearby village of Albu Saif. I realize that were we to hit a landmine, or be targeted by a drone or RPG, it is likely that my bulletproof vest or helmet would not save me from those injuries. I am grateful that Sandra is a medic. She has a greater chance of saving me in the event of an attack than the plates and helmet tucked into the door, mostly worthless but designed to encourage me into places of discomfort such as this.

I ask the driver to stop and I tell my fixer that I want to get out and see the valley below. There's a Humvee wreckage, or what appears to be the hood of the Humvee, and some other debris. The escort ahead doubles back and says there was fighting here and there's a dead body down there and another up on the hill. I say I want to go look and they park on the side of the road, as casually as pulling onto the shoulder of a highway, and I step down onto the trailhead leading to the first body.

Before we go onward, another Humvee arrives and out steps a man who identifies himself as a captain who oversaw the fighting here, and who was based in Albu Saif during the first days of the operation to free East Mosul, where we are now. His lieutenant shoulders an M16 and I follow him to the first body.

I put some distance between me and the lieutenant in the even he steps on a landmine first. I am not wearing my vest or helmet but do not feel exposed. I feel quite light-footed and agile. I point to the bodies I see so that Sandra can start shooting photos. The fixer and the driver, meanwhile, are laughing and jumping around. They are cracking jokes with the privates and are skidding their way down the hill into the valley. It almost seems like they are skiing, horsing around inside a war zone, nearest to the dead bodies of two men. I grow agitated, feeling as though the safety of myself and Sandra is reliant on two juveniles prancing in a minefield. I want to tell them to watch their step but consider whether Sandra and I may be better off if they were blown sky-high.

I try not to focus on them and follow the lieutenant from the first body to the second, which requires us navigating a rabbit trail into the valley. We come across the desiccated remains of an ISIS fighter, his bones tangled in the clothing he wore in the battle that took place here. His skull and jaw and femur soaked in a puddle at the edge of a drainage ditch running beneath the overhead train tracks. Sandra gets close to the bones to photograph them as I make my report and interview the soldiers, who gather around me and are alternately speaking with me and joking with my fixers.

Sandra asks if we can go. Not only is the smell getting to her (oblivious, I can't smell anything) but the fixer and driver are bopping around like Bouncing Bettys. They think this is some game, perhaps they're scared. I am doing my own translating while they watch. I begin to wonder what not being able to smell the stench of death says about me, and my choice in coming to a war zone without any prior experience. I tell the gang that we should leave. I can't tell them why: that I'm frustrated by their inattention, that they are not helping me translate the way I need them to in order to finish my mission, that they are making Sandra uncomfortable. How many times does one need to say something before they are certain it won't ever be heard?

We climb back into the vehicle and I look over at Sandra. We are speeding back toward Erbil and the fixer and driver seem pleased to put the conflict behind them. Their shoulders relax. I ask Sandra if they were making her uncomfortable again, not knowing whether this was normal for war reporters and their fixers and drivers. I do not have a frame of reference but for her own experience, some dozens of months living in Iraq and being with Max, and she tells me that she wasn't uncomfortable per se, but that it was "bad juju" the way they were behaving. I nod my head.

I remind her about Max's Band-Aid and how she was going to tell me about it later. She leans over and whispers that he is covering up a tattoo he got while serving in the Marines in Afghanistan. The tattoo read, "INFIDEL." He has covered it up since coming to Iraq, a matter of precaution.

I lean back into the seat and watch the spoiled desert fade to lush greenery as we near the Kurdish-held territories in the north and, later, Erbil. I am determined to connect myself to what I see, even if I feel apart from my fixer and driver. I learn today that in war there is often an easy disconnect between what is seen and what is felt, like Max's tattoo. As I disembark at my hotel later, I fire my fixer and driver and send them off with a wad of cash. They seem thrilled knowing they can find welfare, even assurance, in the bundle of American dollars.

Over the next several days Sandra and I find a new team to work with and make similar treks to and from Mosul and the surrounding towns and villages, including to the opening day of Qarraqosh where dignitaries flooded the Christian-majority town, which was lined with wooden pews on which pedestrians could sit in the town roundabout, just beyond a checkpoint and its myriad guards. Flippant trash fires burn around the country, almost ornately. Not once do I wear the bulletproof vest or helmet. I never touch the vest or its plates or finger the inside padding of the helmet. They remain brand new, save for the strips of duct tape bearing my blood type in black Sharpie.

Sometimes, when I am back in my hotel room, I close the curtains and make sure no light seeps through. I place my personal satellite tracker beacon on the window ledge and make sure that its green LED indicates its transmissions. I feel seen, watched, looked after. I feel secure and lay down on my bed to stare up at the filthy ceiling and listen to the cars and trucks rumbling outside with the men who are shouting and cursing in a language I cannot understand.

Sandra sends me a text message about our reporting, and we chat briefly before I go off to bed, setting a desk chair against the door, jamming it shut. It is my one hedge against the men shouting outside, in the hallways, harmless though they may be. I fear that the money will run out and the fixer and driver will come kicking in the door searching for more. I trust no one but Sandra.

So it is this way for my entire trip, throughout all the reporting and hundreds of miles driven, the many phone calls I have with sources, and the backroom meetings I have with local officials. Sometimes we drive at night, but very rarely. We stick to roads commonly traveled. I check in with my editor at the end of every day. I phone home to let my then-girlfriend, not yet wife, know that I am back or headed back to the hotel and will soon be home with her, as though I had never left. The cellular and internet services are good so I make calls frequently, text other journalists who I meet at night for drinks, and food, and gossip. All the while, my vest, that expensive and lifesaving device, is somewhere just beyond the fringes of my thoughts and reach. It is for all these reasons that I never touch my body armor, never once tighten the Velcro and plates around me, because a friend and a fixer working to enhance my sight and hearing and voice in a place where senses are rendered useless is a much better barrier against a harmful world, a virtual protective garment bond only as strong as the relationships woven to create it.

4 WHOLLY AROMATIC CARBOCYLIC POLY-CARBONAMIDE FIBER HAVING ORIENTATION ANGLE OF LESS THAN ABOUT 45 DEGREES

The history of Kevlar bulletproofing began in New Kensington, Pennsylvania, a city northeast of Pittsburgh, on July 31, 1923, when Stephanie Kwolek was born to two Polish immigrants. John and Nellie Kwolek raised Stephanie and her younger brother, Stanley, in the scenic city on the bank of the Allegheny River. It was where her father John, a recreational naturalist, would instill in them both an appreciation for science and engender in them a deep love of the natural world.

Stephanie would spend much of her youth swaddled in the wilderness of Western Pennsylvania. She roamed the woods with her father on adventures and naturalist missions during which they sought "animals and snakes and leaves and wild plants" to test their knowledge and see how many they could name. She followed her father's lead, looking for things in the neighboring woods, figuring she might one day follow in the footsteps of her father's interests and his ambitions. "I put all these things in a scrapbook. I, of course, got help from [my father] as to names for all these things and I watched him," Stephanie said in an interview in 2012. Through these woodland adventures under the tutelage of her father, Stephanie learned patience, perseverance, and mindfulness in a world on the brink of collapse.

Stephanie often watched her father read with admiration. She spent her youth helping him garden vegetables and flowers on their land. Stephanie quickly developed an interest in the simple biology of the world she inhabited, the pleasures found and discovered when comfort was in great abundance. So, too, did she learn from her mother, Nellie, a dexterous seamstress who lent to Stephanie's puerile curiosity and growing fascination with things, the way they interact with one another, how fabrics and textiles blend to form sheets and comforters, dresses and undershirts, armor against the weather and the natural world. Years of watching her mother sewing and pattern making left a young Stephanie emulating her mother as she took up the practices of her mother, using the old Singer sewing machine, its needle plunging and threading into and out of cloth and fabric, creating clothes for her toy dolls. She used the same principles learned at the microlevel of her dolls when she began making her own clothing. "I used [my mother's] sewing machine when she wasn't around. It was fun and it was creative and it gave me a great deal of satisfaction," Stephanie once said. She found joy in the practical skills of life and the interweaving of her interests: the need for self-sustaining practices that followed the laws of nature—in the same way that a spider can craft its home by spinning webs, she could create a home within her own clothing designs. These skills proved necessary for a family in the midst of an economic downturn, such as the one ahead of them.

The Great Depression took more from the family than their living wages and future prospects. John died when Stephanie was ten years old. John's death left only Nellie to provide for her family, and she took a job at the local Aluminum Company of America plant, stopping sewing all together. Stephanie had a mother who now worked hard and no longer had time for her, Stephanie said in a media interview. Her ambition for years afterward was to become a fashion designer and Nellie supported this: she knew her daughter, creative and excitable, was a perfectionist and high achiever. Stephanie attended a small school in New Kensington where she quickly shown herself to be academically gifted. Due to the school's size, two grades were taught simultaneously, allowing Stephanie to cram multiple subjects above her grade level. She had inherited her father's extraordinary memory and gift of retention.

Her ability to discover and then retain information, in the same way that she pursued her interests in the natural world and pattern making in her own free time, put

Stephanie ahead of her classroom contemporaries. With sustained grit, her appetite for learning made her stand out from the other students. "This probably made me what I am today," Stephanie told interviewers years later. Because of her immense appetite for work and education, she found herself early on confronted by constant undermining and undervaluing by male students. "If you spoke out of turn, as I did once upon a time, you could make a lot of boys very angry, especially if you knew the answer to a math problem and you spoke up," Stephanie said.

Despite the persistent peer pressure, Stephanie honed an ever-focused attention on her studies during her formative high school years ahead of World War II. This particular moment in history granted women more authority and autonomy in the workforce than ever before, most notably within the defense industry, which saw nearly 350,000 women serving in the armed forces during and after the war.

The conscription of healthy men meant there was greater need for women to enter fields where they had not before been welcome, overseeing everything from running manufacturing plants to joining science, technology, engineering, and mathematics fields. Stephanie saw this opportunity and seized it, enrolling in 1942 as a chemistry major at Margaret Morrison Carnegie College, the women's college associated with Carnegie Mellon University in nearby Pittsburgh.

In college Stephanie revered Dr. Clara Miller who would come to heavily influence Stephanie's journey into adulthood. "It was not an easy time for women then. It surprised me that she was as enthusiastic as she was, and she also was very bright," Stephanie said. She would come to credit Dr. Miller as the most influential figure throughout her college career, surpassing the influence of all other professors combined.

But even those who influenced Stephanie realized that she thrived, without much external inspiration, on her own. Over the summer after her first year at the University of Pittsburgh, Stephanie began a graduate-level position where later her research earned her onto a panel of speakers at the age of nineteen. Stephanie considered herself "green" at the time: young, impressionable, and idealistic, but she also realized that such early interest in her work meant that she "must be pretty good."

In 1946, Stephanie graduated with a bachelor of science in chemistry, specializing in textile chemistry, a blending of all her childhood meanderings. Rather than pursuing her adolescent dream of going into fashion design for fear of frivolous undertakings in financially dire times, Stephanie now dreamed of being a doctor and, after graduating, she sought admission to medical school before realizing the tuition was too expensive.

Stephanie instead decided to build on her undergraduate research. She interviewed with, and received offers from, the Gulf Oil Company and DuPont. Stephanie realized women weren't a first choice for the workforce. The headhunters were merely meeting with her as though she were a curiosity. Few women were being hired and those that were chosen "were hired because there were so few men available. [The men] were at war or just coming back from war, so women were being made offers."

Stephanie accepted the position at DuPont in 1946, shortly after graduating, intrigued by the potential of working for the company that had invented nylon eleven years before. DuPont had become a heavyweight in the field of American science, a company with a presence today in fields ranging from electronics and communications to industrial biosciences, and even protection and sustainable solutions. The company's rich history began in 1802 when French chemist E. I. du Pont brought his knowledge of explosives production to the United States.

By the turn of the century the company had grown, shifted, and evolved from its original business model. In the 20th century, the company's research accolades included perfecting artificial leathers that appeared in automobile interiors, creating synthetic fibers like nylon such as rayon which became staples in commercial fashion. The company even participated in the Manhattan Project, which led to the birth of atomic weapons. The company would over time produce some of the most formidable defense materials ever imagined.

But first, Stephanie had to leave her home in Pennsylvania to begin work at the DuPont facility in Buffalo, New York. Unlike Stephanie, who went on to have a forty-year career as a research scientist at DuPont, many of her female chemistry contemporaries would not stay long. "Particularly women with PhDs in chemistry," Stephanie told interviewers. "They left after about two years and went into teaching."

Over the years, as she watched her female colleagues drop out of scientific fields altogether, Stephanie did not give in to the post-war social pressures placed on women to abandon science. Instead, she decided "to stick it out and see what happened." Her interests in chemistry were reinvigorated. The discoveries she was making at DuPont thrilled her. She became "enamored with the work."

"I would say that I discovered that chemistry was the field that I wanted to be in when I actually started working at DuPont."

Stephanie worked in the Pioneering Research Laboratory of the textile fibers department, focusing almost entirely on polymers, substances that have a molecular structure consisting chiefly or entirely of a large number of similar units bonded together, like fibers, coatings, plastics, and polyurethane. She would spend decades focused on how things come together and form stronger connections.

Stephanie made contributions to fibers still known and used today. In the first two decades of her career, she was part of the advent of Spandex, a fiber developed in 1958, and often woven with other natural and synthetic fibers to give them more elastic qualities. Spandex can be found in everything from stretchy athletic gear like leggings and bicycle shorts to the skintight outfits of '70s and '80s pop idols. She also contributed to the development of Kapton, a polyimide film developed in the 1960s, found in everything from Apollo 11's command module to the tape used in the print table of 3D printers. These fabrics, still used commercially today in everyday lives, held up to the company's commitment to solving "some of the world's biggest challenges."

In 1964, Stephanie and her team were tasked with tackling another one of those global challenges: an impending gasoline shortage. DuPont hoped to discover a strong, lightweight fiber that could replace the wire used in tires in order to improve fuel economy by shedding weight. Despite having spent nearly twenty years as a professional research chemist, this was no small feat for Stephanie. There were many trials and errors as Stephanie toyed with different polymer combinations. She dissolved polyamides in solvents and spun the solutions into fibers, only to have the fibers break during use and stress tests. For a fiber meant for tires, Stephanie and her colleagues could not run the risk of having a tire break or melt on a hot highway after hours of operation in various weather and outdoor conditions.

By 1965, she stumbled upon a revolutionary fiber: poly-paraphenylene terephthalamide. The solution was a combination of a difficult-to-dissolve polymer and an infrequently used solvent. "The solution was very peculiar it was not the typical polymer solution which is sort of like syrup," Stephanie later told an interviewer. "Instead this was a very thin solution, it was watery. Not only was it watery but it was opalescent." Rather than immediately discarding the substance, she asked to try it in the spinneret, which spins fibers out to test their durability.

One of her male co-workers overseeing the spinneret refused to have the substance tested. He believed the fiber would be ineffective and cause damage to the spinneret because of its watery consistency. "Actually, what he was doing was interpreting the opalescence there as particles," Stephanie said. "I filtered this solution and I knew there were no particles in it. And he still refused to spin it."

Stephanie, never one to shy away from having the right answer in a room full of boys, insisted. She knew after hundreds of trials she could have landed on the one combination that might succeed. She had learned that failures were often the best part of the job. The fail, to have no net into which one can fall, is to mean that there are more things to discover and learn. Without failure there was nowhere else to go.

Stephanie needled her male colleague and believed he developed a "guilty conscience" after a few days, at which point he finally agreed. The fiber was tested in the spinneret. "We spun it, and it spun beautifully. It was very strong and very stiff," Kwolek said. The substance was five times stronger than steel by weight and lighter than fiberglass. "I didn't shout 'Eureka,' but I was very excited," Stephanie said.

It took years of further development for the polymer solution to be properly understood and marketed commercially and in 1974 DuPont patented Stephanie's fiber under the name "Wholly Aromatic Carbocylic Polycarbonamide Fiber Having Orientation Angle of Less Than About 45 degrees"—better known today as Kevlar.

It proved an incredibly useful fiber in more ways than initially intended. The fiber, created as a compound to make tires more fuel efficient, was found to have bullet-resistant properties when woven into a fabric and layered several times. Kevlar could protect butchers from their own knives. The fiber could replace the steel in tires and entire boats could be built out of those strands. It could protect law enforcement and military personnel from bullets.

Stephanie retired from DuPont in 1986, ending a four decade career, managing to file more than twenty patents in her name, despite having only a bachelor's degree. During her retirement, Stephanie occasionally consulted for DuPont. She was also known to tutor students, particularly female students, who were interested in science.

Stephanie revolutionized textile chemistry. Some called Stephanie an alchemist, though recognition for her accomplishments came much later. In 1994, she was inducted into the National Inventors Hall of Fame. She was the fourth woman to be inducted out of the hall's 113 recipients. In 1995, Stephanie earned DuPont's Lavoisier Medal for Technical Achievement, which recognizes achievements that "have resulted in significant business impact and enduring scientific value." Through 2014 she was the only woman to have received the award.

She won the Lemelson-MIT Lifetime Achievement Award in 1999. "I find the reaction to my work very satisfying. I also feel like I'm doing some good because when I grew up, I was not exposed to science. I'm always amazed that I did become a chemist and a scientist. I tell young people to reach for the stars and I can't think of a greater high that you could possibly get than by inventing something," she said in an interview with the Lemelson Foundation. In 2003, she was inducted into the National Women's Hall of Fame.

Stephanie died in 2014 at the age of ninety. Her legacy became the discovery of Kevlar which found its way into myriad applications beyond its humble roots of a gas crises. The use of the synthetic fiber is often lost to the colloquialism of the word "Kevlar," now synonymous with weapon shielding and tank armor. In reality, the fibers are meant to join and form a resistance to many of life's demands, not just assailants or enemy gunfire. Kevlar is used in more than 200 applications, including tennis racquets, skis, and parachute lines, and it speaks to true humanity: nothing, not anyone or anything, should stop you in the pursuit of anything that at first seems dangerous, difficult, or insurmountable.

Today, bulletproof vests, also known as ballistic vests or flak jackets, mimic the original concept of the brigandine of the Middle Ages, lining bullet-resistant jackets with metal plates for added protection. Kevlar is also no longer the only option for bulletproofing.

Dyneema and Spectra are recent direct competitors to Kevlar. Made of ultra-high-molecular-weight polyethylene (UHMW/UHMWPE), these fibers are used as composite plates in personal armor and, less frequently, on armored vehicles. Another material that has been used in ballistics vests is Twaron. This para-aramid boasts high heat resistance and is likewise used in sporting goods and protective clothing, which speaks to the much larger importance strength and defense plays in society: as arbiters of well-being and self-soothing.

From its very inception, poly-paraphenylene tereph-thalamide was meant for tires. The strong yet lightweight fiber was Stephanie's creation. In anticipating a gas shortage, she focused her attention on producing a tire that could save on gas mileage. Reflecting on an empowering woman like Stephanie today is necessary, as she and her invention speak to everything brilliant about American manufacturing, research, and development, while simultaneously addressing itself more broadly to our lust for conflict and the desire to protect ourselves—most importantly—at home.

5 PPE FOR YOUR THOUGHTS?

Baghdad, Iraq
January 2019

I travel to conflict areas across the Middle East and North Africa for the next three years. I carry with me my bulletproof vest: to Lebanon, Syria, and Iraq, but I leave my vest in the company of friends while traveling to Israel, Egypt, and Turkey. It is in those countries that I am most fearful of repercussions for traveling with the gear, which has been known to get journalists in the Middle East locked up or worse. It hardly matters. In Israel, I am held for two hours at Ben Gurion Airport and questioned by a young woman who looks like the dozens of women I went to yeshiva with back in Manhattan when I was much younger, more brittle and breakable. I tell her she looks like my sister and that I have family in Jerusalem and that the reason for all the Arabic, Muslim-majority country stamps in my passport is because I'm a journalist.

In Egypt, they're less amenable to my being a journalist and when the guards yank me from the customs line and lead me down a smoke-filled corridor I smile as though they are making a big mistake. I have bought a visa on arrival. I did not want to identify myself as a journalist; the press officers in the airport had caused me a headache for weeks in advance as I tried to get permission so I shrugged them off—and this is what I get. They sit me down next to a weeping woman in a rickety chair and I take deep breaths, about the only thing from my hostile environment training I still use regularly. (I would later come to befriend a doctor of emergency medicine who tells me that everything I learned— the techniques for wrapping a wound and the application of a tourniquet—were worthless and that if someone did not get to a hospital within the Golden Hour it didn't matter what you did, meaning most lifesaving measures were meant to comfort the saver not the saved.) They call it step breathing, as if it's a way to step free of something. I breathe for what feels like a few hours before they let me go.

I have completely abandoned my armored helmet, having since learned that the curvature is meant to deflect glancing bullets more than protect against a direct shot and, since head shots are as hard in real life as I remember them being in the video game Counter-Strike, it has become less of a necessity in my travel-backpack.

What *is* most important these days is my medical bag, newly stocked with a suture kit for deep wounds and several local and oral anesthetics. I also bought a door jammer that fits into a small felt pouch in my hiking bag. The door jammer sits atop the vest. I use it more frequently than the vest and medical bag and believe I need quicker access to it. On a recent trip in Syria, my fixer and driver pull into a hotel at two in the morning and we get small rooms hardly wide enough for one person to stretch out. Before accessing the local Wi-Fi, I slip the door jammer under the door frame. It is shaped like a wedge with a small crankshaft to tighten it to the floor, like a door stop. This is worthless. I turn around to see that there is a balcony and sliding glass door, for which there is no lock, and realize that this safety measure is useless. I fall asleep clutching my chest, as if to hug myself.

I have also, since returning more frequently to the region, become a member of the Frontline Freelance Register. It is a representative body that supports the protection and welfare of its more than 700 members. The body of member-elected officials support war correspondents "who are exposed to risk." It seemed like a good opportunity to grow my network and feel less alone.

I had found the company of many foreign correspondents to be welcoming and helpful. They were eager to give me contacts and advice and this, above all, made me want to be a foreign correspondent. They seemed a family, in a way that did not exist among the crazed mass of journalists working domestically, scooping one another, feigning friendship when practicing tired brinkmanship. I wanted to be part of the something communal and comfortable and, much like many of my other enterprises, I was first rejected. So I traveled to

Mosul that first time somewhat naked, unaccompanied by a support network beyond the personal GPS tracker whose blips and recording points were tracked only by my father and my partner. This, I realize, is the perfect anachronistic painting of a war journalist: Secure in my devotion to the story, insecure from and all the way back home.

Insecurity seems like one form of trauma. I forget that trauma manifests differently in different people. As a freelancer my travels have become overshadowed by a gnawing loneliness. My virtual relationships with editors and publications are easily severable—I have never exchanged more than emails with most of them, never coffee or lunch or phone calls. Four weeks in Syria and two publications, having sent me abroad, seem undisturbed by "killing" one story because of a change in editorship or not responding to emails because . . . well, I'm not sure, since they never responded. The disregard compounds the loneliness, which is never shared openly because such bitterness is socially repulsive. And what with all that was happening in those countries, who are we to complain? Besides, I want future assignments, so I have to seem cheerful, no matter if I spent my recreational and professional days in war zones only to have me and the stories I write forgotten.

I joined the register after my first trip to Mosul hoping the fabric of this international freelance community would be one that could help me in moments like this, curled in my bed in Syria. It seemed like it would be a good opportunity to grow my network and feel less alone, more certain in my abilities to navigate distant, strange lands and complicated logistical planning. Reporting was easy. It was everything that led up to the reporting—the sleepless nights, the travel planning, the insurance premiums that nearly crippled my financial solvency, the difficulty associated with getting assignments and protective insurance—that caused the most strain and difficulty. I wasn't so likely to feel lonely and afraid as I was to feel burned out, depressed, and alone, and as though everyone, from fixers to sources, was against me. Instead I found the calls home, the late-night Skype or WhatsApp conversations were afflicting the very real sense of security I had, knowing that—somewhere, waiting— there were people who were waiting to see me again and wanted me home safe, something I could endanger in others.

The truth was that the best protection and community I had then were my fixers and the few friends I made while reporting, those that I ran into at the offices of press officials as we were getting credentialed across countries such as Syria and Iraq and beyond. I also learned that I am more of an independent operator. I do my best work alone. Perhaps I did not need phone calls with editors or social organizations, letting that external sense of safety form organically.

Before this particular trip to Syria, which I have made from an apartment in Beirut, I called up Nick at bulletproofme. com. I had asked him for a concealable plate carrier, for my ceramic ballistic plates. He did not say he was happy to hear from me, which I had expected from someone who sells protective gear to those headed into war zones. Alas, community is what you make it and he is a businessman. So he sends me a black plate carrier that is meant to go beneath a button-down shirt. I never wear this carrier, either, mostly out of fear of being ridiculed: no one ever seems to wear their vests, not with any regularity, only briefly and when told to by officials. I am in Syria briefly and leave unscathed, returning to my room in Beirut where, like elsewhere, I feel most comfortable when I jam the door with my little blocking device.

On my next trip to Syria I am asked about what gear I have with me at the border. I tell them I have only a pad and pen and a recording device. Nothing more? they ask. Nothing. The vest is more of a burden. It seems to show officials that I am a journalist rather than pronounce my desire to stay safe or alive and as such it is a calling card. Aid workers do not wear them, nor do those serving with medical units treating wounded civilians. I am more often asked about what gear I have with me at any given time than I am ever asked about a press card. And press cards can be made overnight, made seemingly legitimate, given their own weight by a letter of accreditation and perhaps a false rubber stamp. The man ahead of me says he works for a magazine that publishes mostly stories about weed. I suppose anyone with a vest like my own is welcome to places of war.

Months later I travel to Baghdad on a magazine assignment. I will travel throughout central Iraq and Anbar province for about two weeks before taking a domestic flight northward to Erbil, a city I had been to many times since first covering the battle for Mosul. Baghdad is nothing like the pictures I have seen for decades from the American media machine: American soldiers, T-wall barriers, and concertina wire. Just before I arrive the new president pulls down all those barriers and the city feels much like any city in the Middle East: disheveled but for a veiled promise of better days ahead. On my first full afternoon I will come to enjoy a fresh carp, which bobbed in a shallow streetside tub, was bashed over the head by the vendor who then threw it over a fire and served it to my friend—an Agence France-Presse correspondent—and myself as we sat in plastic chairs from which we picked and pawed at the fish's meat using bits of broken taftoon. The night before this lunch, I arrived late, a midnight arrival under darkness being more or less an ineffective part of my security model. I believe that fewer things can be hidden under darkness: streets are less crowded making any predatory activity—from a car, a man—more noticeable. Though I suppose it matters more who I am meeting then who I may never see. It makes me feel safe, this arriving at night, so I do it, whether or not it actually helps I suppose I can only point to my still being here. One exception was in Morocco—a group of streetwise youths following me and my then-girlfriend—that I would rather not recall.

After I land my fixer and I career through the streets outside the Green Zone, passing beneath a bridge bathed in neon lights. Ammar points to the Babylon Hotel, now slipping toward the horizon. He says it is the most expensive hotel in Baghdad, at $350 a night and at which a coffee costs 10,000 Iraqi dinars, roughly $9. "I hate it," he says, one of his favorite refrains, along with "You're high," and "I'm not your girlfriend, man." He says the hotel is so expensive that all you get is a room. "All people think foreigners have much money," I say. "Not me," he says. "I'm different." We drive on along the shoulder of the Tigris River, heading down what Ammar calls the most, or one of the most, expensive streets in Baghdad.

We had talk briefly about the optics of what a man must display in Iraq, how officials care that a man has two nice phones, judge the shoes he wears, and judge the car he drives. I had known since I picked him out at the airport moments before, standing at the aircraft door with a quaffed hair and a faded brown suit, that he cared about appearances. I thought he was from the secret police and had walked on by.

Now we are driving, and Ammar juggles two phones above the steering wheel, castigating me for wearing my seat belt because I at least wanted to get the warning ping to stop while his kept beeping. He tells me that it is going to be suspicious at checkpoints, that I already look Iraqi and should just blend in. He tells me about his girlfriends, says he graduated from Harvard. He says it is expensive to live in Erbil, cheaper in Baghdad, that he can make more money here than in *the States* and can live on $500 a month.

When we pull up to the Agence France-Presse house where I will spend my time in Baghdad, Ammar says, "Let me ask you a question." I think he is going to ask why I have told him I was nervous, which I did a little earlier while we sat and ate kabob at a second-floor restaurant in the darkness of a cool winter night, everyone dressed in hoodies. "No one has ever said that to me before," he said then.

Now he looks at me over the vehicle's center console and says, "Can I have money?" I ask him how much he is asking for and he says, "$200." I tell him, "No, absolutely not." He says, "Thank you." And I say, "No. I said no." He says, "I know. Thank you."

I dart up to my room and use the key he has given me and I lock the door behind me. I put the door jammer in place and breathe a bit easier, but then I think of the possibility that he copied the key and now has access and can come and grab the money he wants and knows I have brought with me to pay him at the end, after our job is done. I tried earlier to tell him I was scared, not of him, but scared in the way I was when I approached the hostile environment instructors in Maryland during my training course years before: as confidants in a dark place, not as a sign of lacking confidence in their or his ability to protect us.

When I did tell him I was scared he became defensive and I found my fear had no place in conversation. Which is why I am sitting on my bed, staring at the ceiling, listening for footsteps in the stairwell, realizing that fear—though reduced through the use of devices such as the GPS locator beacon, bulletproof equipment, and communities whether real or digital—is an emotion better left checked but unspoken.

PPE, this bulletproof equipment, I knew, rarely protects against things as heinous as human intention. The gear is designed only to defend against objects, not people. My gear is fundamentally useless in the practical streetwise situations for which I am supposedly trained or believe myself prepared, like a street-alley kidnapping (I would avoid alleyways) or digital hacking (I wipe my computer clean after each trip). Bulletproof material is only so flexible as to allow fewer thoughts of worry to permeate one's deliberations. Bulletproofing does not protect against backstabbers or fixers and translators who may sell you out to the highest bidder. Bulletproofing is in fact impersonal and rigid, reserved only for the indifference of a bullet.

6 SUPPORT YOUR LOCAL WAR CORRESPONDENT

There is a scene in the movie *Support Your Local Sheriff* that I always remember when in times of serious strife and anxiousness in a combat zone—like that time I was waiting for militia fighters to take my fixer and me to a secure military outpost on the edge of fighting against ISIS, when a soldier from a nearby base, perhaps 200 yards away, fired a round at us, which skipped off the pavement by our Toyota Hi-Lux and zipped into the desert beyond; I thought I saw him smiling, but I couldn't be sure because he was too far away, and I went back to eating my slices of melon, which our driver had carved for us from a fresh cantaloupe. Not wanting to seem disproportionately scared over some jokester having fun, I pretended nothing happened.

The scene I recall from *Support Your Local Sheriff* involves bulletproofing of a kind. It depicts the mayor (Harry Morgan) of an Old West mining town as he tries to recruit a new sheriff (James Garner). The mayor hands the new sheriff the former sheriff's badge, which is marked by a deep bullet crease. Garner looks at it sternly.

"That must have saved the life of the man who was wearing it," the new sheriff says.

"Well it sure would've, Sheriff," the mayor says, half-giddy, "if it hadn't been for all them other bullets flying in from everywhere."

It reminds me of the conversations I imagined editors once had before sending stringers, or freelancers, into combat, a practice that—though still prevalent—is less within the purview of top-tier news organizations. In these conversations they might espouse safety but eschew any responsibility for the newsgatherers under their charge. The scene also reminds me of how deeply a notion of security and safety, how bulletproof materials, or bibles, or flasks, placed just over the heart, can save a life. Perhaps most succinctly, this scene in *Support Your Local Sheriff* reminds me that the notion of something to aid in invincibility is a terribly human fault. That which is meant to make you invincible is rarely certain to work and most definitely will not be painless or without damage—you will, if hit in the small area covered by the ballistics plates or vest, be knocked unconscious or at the very least winded.

At the apex of cultural criticism and comedy, bullet-proofing and Kevlar and its offshoots speak volumes about where humanity sees itself not only at a granular, organic level, but also more globally. We see ourselves as quick, able to outsmart Mother Nature and overcome our enemies—a fallacy of humankind, one largely perpetuated in Hollywood.

In *Sleepy Hollow*, a book given to Ichabod by Katrina stops a bullet from killing him. In *Zorro 2* the priest is shot at and a necklace (with the cross on it) stops the bullet.

In the D-Day scene of *Saving Private Ryan*, a soldier's helmet is clipped by a round from a German MG42. The young soldier takes off his helmet to inspect the spot where the helmet saved his life and another bullet strikes him in the temple, killing him. In *Back to the Future*, at the beginning of the movie, we see Doc Brown (Christopher Lloyd) get shot dead, sparking the catalyst for Marty McFly (Michael J. Fox) to time-travel back to 1955. While there and preparing to head back to the future, Marty warns Doc about what's going to happen to him. The end of the film reveals that Doc heeds Marty's warning and is wearing a bulletproof vest the night he gets shot. (In the third movie, McFly wears a cast-iron stove door to stop a bullet in an old-fashioned Wild West shoot-out.)

In *Kick-Ass*, "Big Daddy" (Nicolas Cage) shoots his young daughter (Chloë Grace Moretz) in the chest to train her to not be scared "when some junkie asshole pulls a Glock." She, of course, is unharmed because she was wearing a bulletproof vest. In *Super Troopers*, a comedy about pot-busting Vermont cops, they test a custom-made bulletproof groin protector. When the cop wearing the cup walks down range and gets hit in the protector, the officer who fired the shot asks how the recipient felt. "Good enough to f**k your mother," he says, his voice strained. In *Mr. and Mrs. Smith*, in the final scene, John and Jane Smith (Brad Pitt, Angelina Jolie) are under fire from operatives that are out to kill them both. They're wearing bulletproof vests, but they rely on each other to keep each other safe.

Batman has all the wealth in the world and is arguably socially and professionally untouchable, but Bruce is willing to drop cold hard cash to feel even more protected in the streets. Even Superman, arguably America's favorite undocumented alien, is bulletproof.

In the penultimate scene of *V for Vendetta*, V is confronted by several secret police and their boss, Mr. Creedy, who has sought to kill him throughout the entire movie. V seems impenetrable to pistol round after pistol round striking his torso, arms, and legs.

"Why won't you die? Why won't you die!"

"Beneath this mask there is more than flesh," an exasperated V says. "Beneath this mask there is an idea, Mr. Creedy. And ideas are bulletproof." V (spoiler alert) kills Mr. Creedy and we see a large steel plate drop from beneath V's robes. Ideas might be bulletproof, or at least infectious, but humans are not and V (spoiler alert) dies from his wounds. The last we see of him is in the hands of a woman he loves. He notes that it is *she* who is the most beautiful thing, forgetting for a moment about his mission and the message that he hopes will carry on in his absence. I like to think that it is that moment he was fighting for all along, an opportunity to say what it was that hid beyond an impenetrable facade.

Meanwhile, I marry my partner. My wife never says it outright, but I hear it in her tone: she'd rather I *not* to go back to a war. She has always encouraged reporting trips, even said she was the reason I got into foreign correspondence and reporting on armed conflict. She used to be a political risk analyst and said her world wonderment had encouraged me by proxy. I tell her she was crazy. I tell her that I love her. I tell her my next trip will be my last and that a month and a half was too long to have one hand at home and another in a distant war zone. I tell her I will come home soon and that I had no plans to return to another war. I meant it half-heartedly. I did not want to take more risks, I say, but it isn't how I really feel.

This was about the time she said, "Good," and I learned I would be a father.

7 A CULT OF ANXIETY

Raqqa, Syria
February 2019

Being bulletproof is no longer a phrase used only in combat and armed conflict. The organic fiber of Kevlar itself, bulletproofing at its most versatile, has become synonymous with not only strength (there's a health supplement and lifestyle brand called "bulletproof," which aims to help "people perform better, think faster, and live better using a proven blend of ancient knowledge and brand new technology"), but safety, despite there being other bulletproofing material often mistaken for Kevlar.

Stephanie Kwolek's Kevlar came to provide much more than military personal armor and combat helmets, ballistic gear, and spall linings inside armored vehicles: to firefighters who wear heat-resistant uniforms reinforced with Kevlar; in body armor is used by police forces; in consumer-grade gloves including the "Ove" Glove is used for cooking over high heat and handling barbecues; in motorcycle riding gear to lessen abrasions in a crash; in lightweight protective jackets and mask bibs for fencing; by speed skaters to protect themselves from skate abrasions if they fall; in the protective blanket that covers horses in bullfighting; basketball shoes; paraglider suspension lines; bicycle tires; table tennis paddles; stringing for tennis racquets; reeds for woodwinds; wicks for fire dancing; brake pads and the bodywork of sports cars like the Ferrari F40; drum heads and several bowed instruments; loudspeaker cones and a roof for the 1976 Summer Olympics in Montreal; wind turbines; smartphones like the Motorola RAZR; Goodyear tires; and DuPont skis. In 2003, DuPont also created a panic room meant for weathering the tornado season.

This growth speaks to society's insatiable need for comfort and protection, even when there is no imminent threat to an individual's body, rather something looming. The comfort is for something less external. It exists within a person's interior.

It may not be bulletproof *per se*, but it borrows from that similar notion of caution and safety in a world filled with danger and existential threats: the anxiety blanket, born of big duvets and heavy sheets. The importance of feeling secure and protected is no longer exclusive to military personnel, law enforcement, or others who may directly be in harm's way. The comforting weight of protective gear is now commercially available as weighted blankets, marketed mostly to those who suffer from anxiety disorders. Dogs and cats have Thundershirts, which act as a drug-free, all-natural treatment for a pet's anxiety by using a weighted vest to mimic "gentle hugging to calm" them. The creator of Thundershirts, for an April Fool's prank, listed a human-sized product on their website and soon their call center was flooded with orders for the fake product.

But those products *are* real.

For humans, there are products like the Huglife Hug, filled with fused quartz beads, that acts as a fourteen-pound weighted blanket "from a desire to help stressed/anxious/scattered clients downshift out of stress response and into the safety and relaxation of 'rest and restore' mode quickly, efficiently, and with very little effort on their part," wrote the blanket's inventor on their Kickstarter page. And *The New York Times* delved into the practice of heavy bedding in an article titled "We Love to Be Smushed," claiming that "weight may be the new thread count."

The science behind anxiety blankets is not new. In fact, the study of the calming effects of an embrace was studied by Temple Grandin, the professor of animal science who, at the age of eighteen, invented her own "squeeze machine." She went on to be the most prominent researcher the field of humane treatment of animals, and later found that putting cattle into ever-decreasing holding areas toward their final stage in the slaughterhouse process made the cattle more calm and pliable, as though a hug is an embrace against death.

In the midst of a month-long reporting trip between Iraq and Syria, I am holed-up in my hotel room in Erbil prepping for the next day—which means I am doing push-ups and jumping-jacks between eating handfuls of beef shawarma while sending WhatsApp messages to my wife—when the photographer assigned to the series sends me a string of frantic text messages about needing her PPE. The photographer says she is stuck in Syria and needs her PPE for our trip, which starts tomorrow. She asks me to meet up with someone who would give her the set she had left in Erbil.

There was a reason she left her gear in Iraq. We were not at first anticipating a visit to the frontline, the last redoubt for ISIS in Syria. The militants were huddled on a postage stamp-sized plot along the border with Iraq and Syria, much farther south than where she was on assignment for an international aid organization. So she did not bring it with her. Then I changed our plans and now she's trying to get her gear ahead of our arrival to ISIS's last stand. Her friend leaves her vest with the concierge at my hotel and I grab it at few minutes later.

It's blue and bulky, with a large neck protector. It weighs nearly twice my own set and is dusty and dirty and smelled of mildew. I cannot find a place for it in my bag, which is already packed with my own vest. For this assignment I have likewise left my helmet at home. I brought my vest only because, well, I did not want to be forced into wearing someone else's heavier, unwieldy set, were we destined to don our gear. This takes some shuffling of food stuffs, electrical components, and the other amenities I've come to bring on these trips, which outstrip any form of bulletproofing material: all the battery power backups, the satellite phone and its accessories, the charging cables for my devices, all of which serve as a better means of protection—methinks—than the bulletproofing that I'm now shoveling into the hiking bag I carry on assignments to the Middle East. I'm thankful I've brought with me the concealable plate carrier and only the front plate. I was not sure how I could fit her PPE if I had brought anything more. Having this extra space is blessing, as I am now able to provide protection for two.

"I had my own, the one I paid for," she is telling me the next afternoon as our driver navigates us away from the border between Iraq and Syria and forces his old SUV, with a cracked windshield, into the Syrian Kurdish mountains of Rojava. The photographer is disappointed. I didn't bring the right gear. More precisely, the friend who delivered the vest to me picked the wrong one. I tell her I am sorry, I should have taken a picture and sent it to her before leaving. Alas, I was too busy with my sandwiches and packing.

"I'll figure it out back in Erbil," she says and adds that she'll have to yell at her husband, whose friend was the one who delivered the wrong vest to me. We sit in silence along the bumpy roads. Verdant green hills clip by at a good pace. The north country of Syria is strikingly beautiful. I see cows and sheep and oil rigs in the distance and I want to take pictures but fear that I will look more like a tourist than a reporter. Besides, as a photographer once told me while we were traveling in Morocco, some things are just for the eyes.

This photographer, a new partner I am working with for the first time, breaks the silence. She is frustrated and now talking at as fast a clip as the scenery is changing outside. A storm cloud breaks overhead and it begins to rain.

"He never trusted me," she says. "He's my husband's best friend in Kurdistan and I bet he sold it." She could not figure out why the vest I brought her was not the one she wanted.

Ever since we first met, he just always looked down on me and I felt always never good enough for him. He was trying to protect my husband, I get that, but I figured if I paid my dues and showed him, I really loved my husband that he would accept me and we could be friends. I think what it *is* is that I stole my husband from him. You know, now we live outside of Kurdistan and have this different life and we don't always return together so I changed everything. I guess my husband agreed to change everything so it's not really my fault, but there always seems to be bad blood there.

She pauses for a moment and stares out the window. I have never been with a photographer who isn't snapping photos until their batteries run dry. She is not. Rather, she is gloomily looking at the clouds and when I think she's about to comment on the weather, how clouds are best for photographing subjects, but a steady rain is not—as though she is pointing out how there is always a middle ground between torrential and tolerable—she says her husband's friend definitely sold it.

"You really think so?" I ask.

"Yeah, I mean, I don't know where else it would be if he couldn't find it."

The vest was important to her because it had her blood type on it—but above all, it was hers, and because it was hers it meant more than if she were to wear someone else's, as though slipping into someone else's skin. She said the whole thing was silly. Of course the patch that denoted her blood type did not matter, because no one in Iraq—none of the fighting forces—would even know what to do with that information. Her relationships were at greater risk of atrophy, something a vest could not protect.

On the way to our hotel, and then onward the next day down to the frontline, and the day after that onto the frontline itself, I tell her we are unlikely to need our vests or helmets and that I, honestly, did not plan on wearing my own.

"I know, but the SDF might make us," she says, referring to the American-backed Kurdish Syrian Democratic Forces who are fighting to oust ISIS.

She is right. We stay the night at an outpost set along an oil field outside the last bouts of fighting. We eat in a crowded mess hall on the base. Tasteless soup, taftoon, and spicy peppers. I eat too many spicy peppers and drink all my soup trying to drown the heat. The warmth from the soup makes everything worse and I go in search of water, stumbling outside into the dark where the stars above form a blanket of disquiet. I walk back to my room, which at first I share with my fixer until he finds a room with his friend. The photographer is in a room in the women's wing and I am sequestered alone. The walls are made of what seems like layers of peeling paint. Two dressers hold a few pillows and some quilted blankets. The mattress pad is no thicker than my thumb. As I turn, I feel every imperfection of the floor.

I cannot sleep, which is not a product of my environment, but rather an affliction I have had since my earliest memory. I toss and turn and listen to the sounds coming from the corridor. A journalist across the hall wheezes. He sounds sick. He coughs and splutters, and I can hear him hit at his laptop keyboard every now and then. His room, I noticed when I passed earlier, has many more blankets and three portable heaters, which is exactly three more than I have in my room. They speak Danish. I look outside my window and see the stars from before. My vest is somewhere nearby, and although there is a risk that the base may be overrun under the cover of darkness, I take a sleeping pill and dream of home.

In the morning, reporters with the Australian Broadcasting Corporation are joshing about, cracking jokes and lighting cigarettes outside their van. A few Bearcats, large armor-plated troop carriers, are idling nearby. A Hi-Lux with a rear-mounted machine gun revs its engine behind them. Farthest back in the convoy is an armor-plated Chevy Tahoe, in which news anchors from Fox News are seated and protected. The security for them seems extravagant, but we know that they are getting special treatment. Where they will be taken, what they are shown, will be a true exclusive for the express purpose of politics. The Kurdish forces are hoping to show President Donald J. Trump, who recently called for the withdrawal of American troops from Syria, that ISIS was still a very real threat and that the Kurds need his support. The Kurds knew that he exclusively watched Fox News and so they got the best rides, the best gear, the biggest scoops.

As Fox News pulls off toward the front line, I watch as the ABC broadcasters are taking selfies in their gear and I imagine them putting those photos on social media and all the comments which will cascade below them: *Be safe out there! Thank you so much for your work! Your mission is very important love you! Be careful and come back! Wow, is that a real vest? Those are some sketchy dudes!* And then the requisite comments in Kurdish and Arabic from the men and women who help those broadcasters, getting them to and from the battlefield without a scratch. The bulletproof vest as a fashion statement, which is another reason I sometimes regard mine as deadweight and nothing more.

Soon we are off in a convoy of our own, traveling not in armored Humvees but a rented van that proves to be a better deterrent than a bulletproof vehicle. Military vehicles, while they may also repel them, attract bullets. It is better to travel seemingly as a group of civilians, which lowers our target profile. We have in the front and back seats two SDF fighters with Kalashnikovs, which, I realize, would be useless were we to come across an Improvised Explosive Device or an ISIS checkpoint—I doubt they would be able to roll down their windows and lift their rifles in a timely enough manner to protect us against a hail of bullets perforating the vehicle.

Which is why I have not put on my vest and instead am keeping it near the door closest to me. Over the last few days, as we have made our way farther and farther south toward where the Euphrates River enters Iraq and where the last of the fighting is happening, my animosity toward my vest and protective gear—the vest, the gas mask, and the potassium iodine tablets—has grown. I imagine all the situations in which any of those would prove most useless.

I remember in Mosul a reporter for a local news station stepping on a landmine and dying from her injuries. Or was it a booby-trapped mass grave? I remember a group of coalition soldiers, tailed by reporters, encircling a fallen ISIS fighter in a field who blows himself up when they get near. I remember the stories of journalists secluded in a residential building inside Mosul where they slept with the vest on and were crushed when a Vehicle-Born Improvised Explosive Device crashed into the side of their building and detonated. All were wearing body armor. I think of the kidnapped journalists who are beheaded and of the ones who were struck by friendly fire. I think of all this and know that the only moments I felt safe were not when I was in any particular gear, and not with any particular satellite tracking device, but those times when I was with people who felt as I did and we responded to one another's discomfort. It also seemed that those moments of terror come quicker than one might be able to respond with any effective countermeasures. Wearing a vest at all times is, however, impractical. So it sits out most action.

I remember interviewing a family outside Kirkuk, in a beautiful house with an old Soviet rifle mounted above the fireplace. The host and his wife invited me to stay the night to save us the long drive back to Erbil until morning. I decided against staying, even though my fixer was tired and felt the drive home would be too exhausting. It was a good decision, as the next morning, when I awakened in my room in Erbil, I learned that a suicide bomb attack in the town where we would have stayed killed nearly a dozen people.

As we reach the frontline we have still not put on our vests and as we make our way back later in the day the gear lies dormant in the backseat of the van.

I hate interviewing civilians struggling to lift the boulders and wreckage of their former life while I stand by wearing bulletproof armor. It seems to me a contrast of ideas and hope: where they feel safe enough to rebuild, I stand in complete protection asking them whether they feel safe to rebuild. Our ideas of safety are different. Theirs is in the absence of something—ISIS—while mine is in the presence of a strong support team and access to the internet, through which connection I might dial my wife. Of course, it is when the fixers and interpreters get lost or angry, when I am unable to reach my wife, that things feel askew and dangerous. Otherwise the days slip by unattended.

In truth there was both safety and danger in the presence of our security team, ragtag though it was. As I stand on a deserted roadway and interview residents without military guard, a way of operating without oversight in the grey area between protection and recklessness, I realize that, by virtue of their standing there, of them riding their motorbikes freely, I can at the very least be certain *they* are certain of their safety. Whether or not I knew whether their allegiances lie with ISIS or the SDF, I can be certain that they are freely mobile and that, in their tracks, I can walk somewhat more securely. They would not be outside, walking and driving, were there threats. Of course, there are instances when crowded spaces are potential targets for violence, but since shedding my military minders I feel less burdened by my own alien presence and the possibility of a random attack. At worst I could be mugged and that was why my fixer was standing with me translating as we went: he could negotiate his way out of just about anything.

The same goes for my friends in Erbil, who are waiting for me to cross back into Iraq from Syria. My journey into and out of Syria, then Iraq, is always straightforward. Like the last time, I drive north on what remained of Highway 6, turning east at Ain al-Issa and onto the M4. Through dozens of checkpoints I make my way back to the ferry crossing into Northern Iraq where on the other side my friend picks me up. We drive to a small roadside shanty and share a Buzz mango vodka mixed drink and another pack of cigarettes. We cruise into the city of Erbil, order takeout or visit with his family in the mountains to the south, and talk into the night about our hopes and dreams for the future. He wants to reopen a restaurant, maybe work at a local media outlet. I want to publish a book, maybe two. He would give me a list of Kurdish names for my child, which I learn in Syria will be a boy. And the new life, the opportunities ahead, glimmer, a pmirage on the horizon.

By his side I felt that I could go anywhere.

8 SAFETY IS A CABIN IN THE WOODS

New England
April 2019

We are likely to welcome things that frighten us if at first we have a foundation of comfort and safety from which to receive them.

My last trip, to Raqqa, Syria, is a dream. I have learned during my travels that I will be a father and, when I land at Boston Logan International Airport, I cry at the first sight of an American flag. I am never this precious or homesick, never so enraptured by a symbol of manufactured safety and security, fleeting though it proves to be.

Funny, the way things vanish. I am stopped by a border patrol agent and taken with a group of travelers who are coming from Turkey and other Muslim-majority countries, travelers who are sleepy and dark-skinned, like me. We are separated, over thirty long and cautionary minutes, into ever smaller groups until I am standing alone before a man with a backward baseball cap and a golden badge strung from his neck. He has the build of someone once in the military.

"Where are you coming from?" the agent asks, not looking up from his paper.

"Istanbul," I say, pronouncing the Turkish capital as an American and not with an accent as normally I would, a habit I have developed to afford me a bit of credibility, or care, while traveling outside my comfort zone, away from friends and family.

"Anywhere else?"

I tell him my trip had originated in Iraq and he asks where in Iraq and I tell him Baghdad and he asks anywhere else. I tell him I traveled to Anbar Province, along the border with Syria. He asks if I entered Syria.

"I did," I say. I peer over the rostrum and watch him notate everything I say. I heave. It is exhaustion. I am tired and I know what comes next, like Egypt and Israel, will not end quickly. It will drag on and I hate the anticipation. No bulletproofing can defend against interrogation. Wit or calm is a better defense. In my case, I am nonchalant.

"Where did you go?"

And the conversation goes on, into further details of my travel, getting specific about the locations I visited, and the people with whom I met, and the hotels in which I stayed. As the questioning continue, I become more fearful, feeling as though I am naked and standing out in the open, exposed. I think of my Kevlar vest in my backpack.

"Is it my turn to ask questions?" I say as he begins to encroach on information—about sources, people, information I had not yet published through my newsgathering—that I am unwilling to share and flat out will not. He stops short and says, "Sure, what do you want to know?"

"What's the difference between the two groups you split us into?"

"That I cannot tell you."

"All right, then why are all of us being singled-out. Seems reckless, but also abnormal. I've flown into Boston half a dozen times with this passport, Arabic stamps included, and have never been stopped."

He tells me there's some algorithm that flagged me and the others, a computer that decided my travel was suspicious and hence, he said, the interrogator. He tells me to wait and left me standing alone by his station. In a few minutes he returns.

"You went to Columbia and Harvard? You work for *The New York Times*?"

"Your intelligence collection is a combination of LinkedIn and Google, then?" I say, maintaining some semblance of cheer against my fatigue. "Look, man, if we're done here I gotta get going. My pregnant wife is waiting for me and I'm tired as shit."

"Yeah, that's all right. But what are you doing in these places?" He has stopped taking notes, his handwriting having filled an entire sheet on his yellow legal pad. Another officer, who seems to have finished his shift, stood in a hooded sweatshirt aside the other officer, arms akimbo. "Yeah, my buddy was over there—fighting, later as a journalist—and says it's a mess, a downright sandbox of shit."

It was a difficult place, but not an impossible place to understand. I tell them I think it is easy to perceive it as nothing but a terrible, fraught, and dangerous place, given our relationship to it as Americans. I point to a recent article in *The Times* travel section about visiting the mountains of Northern Iraq. I say it is getting better and that, despite the news, there's hope for the region. Perhaps not in five years, but when the generation in which I was born begins taking Congressional seats (as is happening) and leaders of other nations are replaced by adults who tired of politics and religion dictating policy, things can change. I remain ever doe-eyed, at least in speaking about the wars with outsiders. It is, in a small way, my hope to de-escalate the questioning, but also to share a thoughtful experience of the Middle East—not one marked by blood and bombs. I am also aware of my own ignorance in these matters. Rather than answer their questions, I just think back to my wife, sitting in our car not 100 yards away, how desperate I am to see her and turn my back against death.

"You're crazy," the officer tells me. "I'd be scared, fuck that. Weren't you?"

Their unwinding demeanor feels a lot like my time with American soldiers, at home and abroad. It has a boyish quality of curious disgust, the way a child might examine an earthworm before killing it. Truth was, I was more scared of them, standing there in their bulletproof vests with their handguns, and badges, and the unimaginable quantity of outcomes over my life that they held, than I was scared of the people who, in Syria and Iraq, were gracious enough to let me into their homes, cook me meals, and share their stories, to protect me when language and cultures were barriers overcome by words, not bullets.

Standing before me I am more certain that the lectern, their badges, their fear born of years watching media reports about the violent, uncontrollable Middle East, could more quickly destabilize my life than an encounter with a rogue militia overseas. In this moment it is not my vest that can protect me, but rather a cheerful demeanor meant to connect and bridge, not distance, which is what the vest always seemed to do while I was reporting.

I awaken in a cottage in the woods. I had spent the last two nights with my wife in hotels in southern New Hampshire where I was about to begin a writing residency. Now I am alone in my bed. It is five in the morning and a radio alarm clock whispers the morning news. A woman says, "Sometimes we get stuck in our past and let our past guide us," as I poke my feet into a pair of slippers beneath the bed. I flip on the thermo pot. In the fireplace the night before I made a nest of birch bark and small twigs beneath sturdy logs. The hearth is wide and gives me space to maneuver a match into the small bed of kindling. It comes alive and I stare into the smoke curling upward and outside to the world. I wash my hands, run a brush across my teeth, grin into a mirror, and splash my face with water. The last part of my routine, before I turn off the radio, pour a cup of tea, and sit down to write, is to reach the front door and uncurl the door jammer from its perch against the door jamb. It has watched over me as I slept, even when settled in a place like home. Some mornings I believe the device has moved slightly, that someone tried kicking the door. No one ever has.

This worry is habitual, the placement of the door jammer necessary. I started using it frequently when dead bolts and chains seemed terrible, ineffective ways to lock a door. It was all of a few ounces and took up less space than my vest. It was small and red and perfect in its discretion. That is the hallmark of something that protects as it does not ward off outsiders the way a vest might, the way the bulge beneath a T-shirt screams of a large and inescapable worry. I think of the time that Jared Kushner wore one and was mocked for making it seem like an accessory rather than a material to keep him alive. Beneath that was an insecurity stretching beyond the discomfort associated with thoughts of death. And I think about the ways I always twitched for my own vest, unsure if the moment I needed it was near, or if it was a fabrication in my head. No one has caught me, yet, using the jammer, of which I am also ashamed but know that it is easily hidden. If anyone asked—they never do—what it was I had dangling from a pouch on the door handle, I'd tell them it was something to help me sleep at night.

I never sleep well regardless, but I suppose having the jammer there buys me time to clear the sand from the crooks of my eyes before I am taken, or beaten, or any number of awful things. I have always said that the most frightening thing about being in the woods is not the solemnity of being alone, but the notion that you may have company.

Where my slippers were, I have also hidden my trauma first aid kit, my medical pack, my vest, and my gas mask with filter and potassium iodine tablets for protection against areas contaminated by chemical weapons attacks. These things aren't needed, but I have not yet returned home so still they are carried with me. I sit down at my desk and the steam unfurling off the tea fogs my glasses.

The rising sun paints the sky and its clouds orange. I decide on a hike and swing on my backpack, prepping for the trek through the wilderness. I do things out of order, uncertain of everything, feeling a bit lost now that I have nothing to worry about and no inherent fear. It is the absence of fear that makes me worry. It feels like I am perhaps forgetting something that, in its absence, I will be harmed for forgetting. The backpack feels good, and the boots fit snug around my ankles, and the hat on my head is held tightly by the band of the headlamp casting a beam through the doorway into the early morning darkness, my backpack hugging me—empty except for its empty weight, which feels to me like a shield.

After learning I will become a father, I recall how the children in Raqqa played between the holes bored through buildings and first used as passageways by ISIS. I remember how people were made to disappear and taken by way of the holes; but also how much fun chasing a friend through them might be. The world through a child's eyes, no matter the battlefield, can always be a playground. Though with that innocence come the families halved by loss and displacement, the amputated children who stooped to grab a shimmering promise of a buried toy that was instead an explosive. So at night, when I take my walks, I focus on my footing, as I did while overseas. I stepped not freely but only on the safely trodden paths of those who came before me. I thread through the birch and pine. If I forget my bag, in its absence I turn frequently, jumping at the wind, or a leaf relieved of its perch. David Foster Wallace once noted that his bandana was much like a security blanket, calling it a foible—a nod and recognition of an inherent weakness. It is this way with my backpack and the headlamp that guides my way in the evenings or early mornings such as this. It is impossible that something might be here in this ankle-high snow, waiting to attack, a sure fallacy that the roads could be lined with improvised explosive devices, causing my step to be more lively. After a few days, I learn to sometimes forgo these things that were once necessities. I trek the forest alone, winding through wicked paths of ice and snow, without a backpack or headlamp, but carrying with me a resilience that comes only with learned caution.

Yet from time to time I still seek the protection of these things—the backpack like a security blanket at my rear, the light shining to illuminate a constant darkness—because being equipped with the right tools, emotional and physical, may not make me bulletproof. At best it makes navigating the world less daunting, but rather something pleasing.

When I disengage the bolted front door, it signals for me the start of the day. I can remember that which haunts me, and that from which I must protect myself. It does well to be impeccable and careful with your words, cautious with strangers, wary of what insights you glean from your gut. But beyond that, the best one can do is hope. Set free the lock and, hands trembling though they may be, step into the wild world, for it beckons.

REFERENCES

Chapter 1

Article 4 A (1, 2, 3 and 6) of the Third Geneva Convention and Article 79 of Additional Protocol I.

Addario, L. (2015). *It's What I Do: A Photographer's Life of Love and War*. London: Hachette UK.

ISIS Video Purports to Show Beheading of James Foley. (2017, December 20). Retrieved from https://www.nytimes.com/2014/08/20/world/middleeast/isis-james-foley-syria-execution.html.

Leaked US Video Shows Deaths of Reuters' Iraqi Staffers. (2010, April 6). Retrieved from https://www.reuters.com/article/us-iraq-usa-journalists/leaked-u-s-video-shows-deaths-of-reuters-iraqi-staffers-idUSTRE6344FW20100406.

Schmitt, E. (2009, September 9). Seized Times Reporter Is Freed in Afghan Raid that Kills Aide. Retrieved from https://www.nytimes.com/2009/09/09/world/asia/09rescue.html.

Chapter 2

Armor Types—Different Types of Armour by Historical Period. (n.d.). Retrieved from http://www.historyofarmor.com/armor-facts/types-of-armor/.

armour | History, Types, Definition, & Facts. (n.d.). Retrieved from https://www.britannica.com/topic/armour-protective-clothing.

Author: Dirk H. Breiding. (n.d.). Arms and Armor: Common Misconceptions and Frequently Asked Questions | Essay | Heilbrunn Timeline of Art History | The Metropolitan Museum of Art. Retrieved from https://www.metmuseum.org/toah/hd/aams/hd_aams.htm.

Authors: Seán Hemingway, Colette Hemingway. (n.d.). Mycenaean Civilization | Essay | Heilbrunn Timeline of Art History | The Metropolitan Museum of Art. Retrieved from https://www.metmuseum.org/toah/hd/myce/hd_myce.htm.

Aztec Warfare. (2015, March 18). Retrieved from https://www.ancient.eu/Aztec_Warfare/.

Aztec Warriors: Weapons and Armor. (2018, June 14). Retrieved from https://www.historyonthenet.com/aztec-warriors-weapons-and-armor.

BulletProofME.com Body Armor / Bullet Proof Vests. (n.d.). Retrieved from https://www.bulletproofme.com/.

Chain mail. (n.d.). Retrieved from https://www.britannica.com/technology/chain-mail.

Chain Mail. (n.d.). Retrieved from http://www.medieval-life-and-times.info/medieval-swords-and-armor/chain-mail.htm.

Chainmail Armour. (n.d.). Retrieved from http://www.medieval-chronicles.com/medieval-armour/chainmail-armour/.

Cuirass. (n.d.). Retrieved from https://www.britannica.com/technology/cuirass.

Edwards, P. (2015, August 5). Why Ancient Armor Had Awesome Abs. Retrieved from https://www.vox.com/2015/8/5/9097165/ancient-greek-abs.

History.com (2018, August 21). Sumer. Retrieved from https://www.history.com/topics/ancient-middle-east/sumer.

The History of Body Armor, From Medieval Times to Today. (n.d.). Retrieved from https://smallwarsjournal.com/jrnl/art/the-history-of-body-armor-from-medieval-times-to-today.

How Shall a Man Be Armed? Evolution of Armor during the Hundred Years War. (2015, September 15). Retrieved from http://www.medievalists.net/2013/10/how-shall-a-man-be-armed-evolution-of-armor-during-the-hundred-years-war.

Knighton, A. (2017, July 4). The Development of Armor—From Ancient Times to Modern Warfare. Retrieved from https://www.warhistoryonline.com/history/9-key-stages-development-armor-m.html.

Light, Mobile, and Many: Rethinking the Future of Armor. (2019, January 2). Retrieved from https://mwi.usma.edu/light-mobile-many-rethinking-future-armor.

Medieval Chainmail Armor History. (n.d.). Retrieved from https://www.knightsedge.com/s-8-chainmail.aspx.

Medieval Welfare.com (n.d.). Medieval Armour. Retrieved from http://www.medievalwarfare.info/armour.htm.

Mesopotamia II Notes. (n.d.). Retrieved from http://www3.northern.edu/marmorsa/mesopotamia2notes.htm.

Mycenaeans: 10 Things You Should Know About the Bronze Age Greeks. (2019, April 25). Retrieved from https://www.realmofhistory.com/2016/05/23/10-incredible-facts-mycenaean-armies.

Suit of Armor. (n.d.). Retrieved from https://www.knightsedge.com/s-7-suit-of-armor.aspx.

Sumer. (n.d.). Retrieved from https://www.britannica.com/place/Sumer.

Tailored to the Times: The Story of Casimir Zeglen's Silk Bullet-Proof Vest. (n.d.). Retrieved from https://www.academia.edu/8701355/Tailored_to_the_Times_The_Story_of_Casimir_Zeglens_Silk_Bullet-Proof_Vest.

Warfare History Network. How the Cannon Marked the End of the Knight's Suit of Armor. (n.d.). Retrieved from https://warfarehistorynetwork.com/daily/military-history/how-the-cannon-marked-the-end-of-the-knights-suit-of-armor.

https://www.thetrace.org/rounds/mass-shooting-gun-type-data.
https://www.washingtonpost.com/graphics/2018/national/
    mass-shootings-in-america/?noredirect=on&utm_
    term=.9bb91fde5f48.
https://www.cga.ct.gov/2013/rpt/2013-R-0057.htm.

Chapter 3

Al Jazeera. ISIL Attacks Police Station near Mosul. *Iraq
    News | Al Jazeera*, Al Jazeera (2017, April 23). www.
    aljazeera.com/news/2017/04/isil-attacks-police-station-
    mosul-170423092506161.html.
Mission. (n.d.). Retrieved from http://www.frontlinefreelance.org/
    mission.

Chapter 4

1999 *Lemelson-MIT Lifetime Achievement Award Winner Stephanie
    L. Kwolek* [Video file]. (2009, February 28). Retrieved from
    https://www.youtube.com/watch?v=8dX3Z5CyF3c.
About.com. (n.d.). WebCite query result. Retrieved from
    https://www.webcitation.org/query?url=http%3A%2F%2F
    inventors.about.com%2Flibrary%2Finventors%2Fblkevlar.
    htm&date=2009-05-24.
About Us. (n.d.). Retrieved from https://www.dupont.com/
    corporate-functions/our-company.html.
American women and World War II. (n.d.). Retrieved from
    https://www.khanacademy.org/humanities/us-history/rise-to-
    world-power/us-wwii/a/american-women-and-world-war-ii.

Bw6707. (n.d.). Kevlar® aramid fiber USA. Retrieved from http://www.dupont.com/products-and-services/fabrics-fibers-nonwovens/fibers/brands/kevlar.html.

Carlson, M. (2017, November 30). Stephanie Kwolek obituary. Retrieved from https://www.theguardian.com/science/2014/jun/26/stephanie-kwolek.

The History of DuPont Kevlar. (n.d.). Retrieved from https://www.safeguardclothing.com/articles/the-history-of-kevlar.

How Does Kevlar Work? | Why Is Kevlar So Strong? (2018, April 23). Retrieved from https://www.explainthatstuff.com/kevlar.html.

How One "Failure" Changed the World: The Story of Kevlar. (n.d.). Retrieved from http://www.edgeofyesterday.com/time-travelers/how-one-failure-changed-the-world-the-story-of-kevlar.

Innovative Lives: Stephanie Kwolek and Kevlar®, The Wonder Fiber. (2016, June 23). Retrieved from http://invention.si.edu/innovative-lives-stephanie-kwolek-and-kevlar-wonder-fiber.

Kevlar Inventor Stephanie Kwolek, 90, Dies. (2014, June 20). Retrieved from https://www.usatoday.com/story/money/business/2014/06/20/kevlar-inventor-stephanie-kwolek-dies/11133717.

Legacy of Distinction. (2006, June 1). Retrieved from https://www.cmu.edu/cmtoday/issues/june-2006-issue/feature-stories/legacy-of-distinction/

Martin, D. (2009, December 2). Lester Shubin, 84; Used Kevlar in Vests, Saving Lives. Retrieved from https://www.nytimes.com/2009/12/03/us/03shubin.html

Mothers of Invention: Stephanie Kwolek. (2019, January 21). Retrieved from https://digging-history.com/2014/08/11/mothers-of-invention-stephanie-kwolek/

PROTECTING THOSE WHO PROTECT US: THE
    BULLETPROOF VEST PARTNERSHIP GRANT PROGRAM.
    (n.d.). Full text. Retrieved from https://archive.org/stream/gov.
    gpo.fdsys.CHRG-112shrg73812/CHRG-112shrg73812_djvu.txt.
Quinn, J. (2003). AmericanHeritage.com. Retrieved from https://
    www.webcitation.org/5h0Ix9E2E.
Remembering Inventor Stephanie Kwolek. (n.d.). Retrieved
    from http://lemelson.mit.edu/news/remembering-inventor-
    stephanie-kwolek.
The Science Behind 4 of the Greatest Polymers of All Time.
    (n.d.). Retrieved from https://www.popsci.com/science/
    article/2012-11/science-behind-4-greatest-polymer-
    inventions-all-time.
Smith, Kiona N. (2018, August 1). Stronger Than Steel: How
    Chemist Stephanie Kwolek Invented Kevlar. Retrieved from
    https://www.forbes.com/sites/kionasmith/2018/07/31/
    stronger-than-steel-how-chemist-stephanie-kwolek-invented-
    kevlar/#46c6a0e21c3e.
Stephanie Kwolek (1923–2014). (n.d.). Retrieved from https://
    www.acs.org/content/acs/en/education/whatischemistry/
    women-scientists/stephanie-kwolek.html.
Stephanie Kwolek. (n.d.). Retrieved from https://www.
    ericksonliving.com/tribune/articles/2015/08/stephanie-kwolek.
Stephanie Kwolek. (n.d.). Retrieved from http://lemelson.mit.edu/
    resources/stephanie-kwolek.
Stephanie Kwolek. (n.d.). Retrieved from http://lemelson.mit.edu/
    winners/stephanie-kwolek.
Stephanie L. Kwolek. (2017, December 9). Retrieved from https://
    www.sciencehistory.org/historical-profile/stephanie-l-kwolek.
Stephanie L. Kwolek. (2017, December 9). Retrieved from https://
    www.sciencehistory.org/historical-profile/stephanie-l-kwolek.

Stephanie Kwolek | 175 Faces of Chemistry. (n.d.). Retrieved from http://www.rsc.org/diversity/175-faces/all-faces/stephanie-kwolek.

Stephanie Kwolek: Inventor of Kevlar®. (n.d.). Retrieved from http://www.women-inventors.com/Stephanie-Kwolek.asp.

Stephanie L. Kwolek, Inventor of Kevlar, Is Dead at 90. (2017, December 20). Retrieved from https://www.nytimes.com/2014/06/21/business/stephanie-l-kwolek-inventor-of-kevlar-is-dead-at-90.html.

Stephanie Kwolek: Kevlar® Inventor. (2018, March 28). Retrieved from http://invention.si.edu/stephanie-kwolek-kevlar-inventor.

Stephanie Kwolek, Kevlar Inventor, Dead at 90. (n.d.). Retrieved from https://www.popsci.com/article/science/stephanie-kwolek-kevlar-inventor-dead-90.

The Washington Post. Retrieved from https://www.washingtonpost.com/national/stephanie-kwolek-dies-at-90-chemist-created-kevlar-fiber-used-in-bullet-resistant-gear/2014/06/20/9b5b4634-f883-11e3-a606-946fd632f9f1_story.html.

Woman Who Invented Kevlar Dies. (2014, June 21). Retrieved from https://www.bbc.com/news/world-us-canada-27951043.

Women in Chemistry. (2018, April 24). Retrieved from https://www.sciencehistory.org/learn/women-in-chemistry.

Women in Chemistry: Stephanie Kwolek [Video file]. (2012, September 10). Retrieved from https://www.youtube.com/watch?v=L1pepaAdkWA.

Chapter 5

Lands of Metamorphosis. *Pacific Standard* (2018, May 7). psmag.com/social-justice/lands-of-metamorphosis.

Chapter 6

Alien Nation
Back to the Future
Back to the Future III
Batman Begins
Black Hawk Down
Dark Knight
The Departed
John Wick
Kick-Ass
Lord of the Rings
Missing in Action
Mr. & Mrs. Smith
R.I.P.D.
Saving Private Ryan
Snakes on a Plane
Superman Returns
Super Troopers
Support Your Local Sheriff
Training Day
Twin Peaks
V for Vendetta

Chapter 7

About Bulletproof. *Bulletproof*, www.bulletproof.com/pages/about-us.
Huglife—The Next Generation Weighted Blanket. (n.d.). Retrieved
from https://www.kickstarter.com/projects/huglifehug/huglife-
the-next-generation-weighted-blanket?fbclid=IwAR0rNAxdY

JGEtKpHxMAPWXqoefRgSepShIHjSoBG3GD3jAPmme5Qq
GNGtBw.

Iraq: Fresh Evidence that Tens of Thousands Forced to Flee
Tuz Khurmatu amid Indiscriminate Attacks, Lootings and
Arson. Amnesty International, www.amnesty.org/en/latest/
news/2017/10/iraq-fresh-evidence-that-tens-of-thousands-
forced-to-flee-tuz-khurmatu-amid-indiscriminate-attacks-
lootings-and-arson.

The Many Uses of Kevlar. (n.d.). Retrieved from https://www.
safeguardarmor.com/uk/articles/kevlar-uses.

ThunderShirt for Humans | ThunderWorks. (n.d.). Retrieved from
https://www.thundershirt.com/humans.html.

We Love To Be Smushed. (2019, February 25). Retrieved from
https://www.nytimes.com/2019/02/23/style/weighted-blankets-
sleep.html.

Workflow-Process-Service. (n.d.). Consumer Products Made
with Kevlar® | Kevlar® Fiber USA. Retrieved from http://www.
dupont.com/products-and-services/fabrics-fibers-nonwovens/
fibers/uses-and-applications/consumer-products-kevlar.html.

Workflow-Process-Service. (n.d.). Aerospace, Marine, & Rail
| DuPont USA. DuPont, www.dupont.com/products-
and-services/fabrics-fibers-nonwovens/fibers/uses-and-
applications/aerospace-marine-rail.html.

Chapter 8

MacDowell Colony. The Portable MacDowell. portablemacdowell.
org/#artists/kenneth-r-rosen.

ACKNOWLEDGMENTS

Many thanks to: The MacDowell Colony for their generous support, Halo Aziz, Tim Arango, Seyward Darby, Sarah Fallon, Frank Huyler, Kimberly Meyer, Luke Mogelson, Michael Scott Moore, Haaris Naqvi, Sabrina Negrón, Tekendra Parmar, Evan Ratliff, Mark Robertson, Christopher Schaberg, Ian Urbina, the editors at *Anxy* and *The Delacorte Review* (in which portions of this work originally appeared in different forms), the many fixers, interpreters, and drivers whose names are withheld for security reasons (like some of the names in this book, which have been changed), and to my family, for their encouragement and understanding throughout my travels into distant, unknown lands.

INDEX